# Cockatiel

## Cockatiels as Pets

### Cockatiel book for care, costs, feeding, health, grooming and training.

By

Louis Vine

# Table of Contents

# Introduction

Who can resist the adorable charm and sweet disposition of cockatiels? Many of the endearing qualities existing in other animals can be readily found in a well handled "tiel". If you want a pet bird that will happily perch on your shoulder, one who craves your company and voice, a bird to have as a friend for years to come, then a cockatiel is for you.

Cockatiels that are allowed to live in the sort of environment where its highly sociable and inquisitive nature thrives make some of the best pets around. Their small size gives bird lovers living in any home the chance to own a pet. Even a small studio apartment that is properly equipped can make a wonderful home for these birds.

If you're the type of pet owner who's looking for an intelligent creature that will require bonding time and return affection lovingly, then look no further than cockatiels. On the other hand, if you prefer a pet you can admire from afar but not have to interact with, these birds aren't for you. Cockatiels have an innate desire to bond with others, to learn new things and to receive and give friendship.

This book will teach you everything you need to know to create a home that will make any cockatiel chirp happily. With patience and dedication, you can have a pet that seeks your company much like a puppy, enjoys being pet like a kitten, and is an unforgettable bird that will continually entertain you with its unique blend of playful antics.

# Chapter 1. Cockatiels As Pets

Cockatiels make wonderful pets. These birds have delightful personalities and each cockatiel has its own unique set of traits, making these creatures far more interesting. Any cockatiel pet owner will tell you their feathered friend can rival the antics of other birds, including other species of parrots (cockatiels are a type of parrot) and their cousin, the cockatoo. The charm and playful characteristics of "tiels" make them one of the most popular pet birds in the world.

These little heartbreakers are the second most popular pet bird around, second only to parakeets. With their adorable orange cheek patches and inquisitive and playful demeanor, it's easy to see why. A well-handled bird can greet you with kisses, perch on your shoulders as you watch TV or go about your daily tasks, and even come when called. Many cockatiels can mimic human words. These birds will typically act excited when they see their owners, much like a happy puppy would.

There's so much to love about these creatures. Owning one will add joy and laughter to your home, provided your own lifestyle and personality matches that of a good cockatiel pet owner.

# 1.   Making An Important Decision

But is owning a pet cockatiel right for you? Just like no dog is the perfect match for any type of dog-lover (some are too energetic to live in an apartment, while other dogs don't have the right temperament for small children) not everyone has the lifestyle, time, preference and personality that match that of a responsible cockatiel handler.

Here are several key things you need to know about cockatiels to help you decide if you can provide the environment it needs to lead a healthy and happy life:

- **High energy level.** Cockatiels are, without a doubt, active birds. They require plenty of stimulation and may begin to exhibit destructive behavior—such as plucking their own feathers—when they get too bored. You, the owner, should have time each day to spend with your cockatiel. Your activities together could be as simple as watching TV with the bird by your side, or spending some time each day reading aloud to your pet. Because cockatiels are high-energy pets, they require a spacious birdcage. The minimum recommended cage size should have a dimension of 24" x 24". Your bird will need bird toys and pet perches to keep it occupied and mentally stimulated.

- **Lengthy Lifespan.** Owning a pet cockatiel means making a commitment spanning over a decade or even more. When kept in captivity, these creatures can live for an average span of 15 to 20 years. Sometimes it can be as short as 12 years— still a long time to commit to a pet! There are reports of cockatiels that lived for 30 years and even longer.

**Requires bonding and training.** Perhaps you're thinking of acquiring a pet cockatiel because you saw a friend's bird hop on a finger and give its owner kisses. Maybe your young child saw a tamed bird on TV and is now begging for one of his own. Keep in mind that cockatiels are intelligent creatures with unique personalities. Not all cockatiels behave alike. In addition, don't expect to bring home a new pet cockatiel and have it act as sweet as a purring kitten off the bat. Earning the bird's trust will take time and patience. In most cases, you will have to put in hours and hours of bonding with a cockatiel before it begins to behave affectionately. Some birds even react violently at first, especially in the cases of older cockatiels who weren't taught to bond with humans at an early age.

- **They can bite.** Though it's not difficult with time and patience to tame a cockatiel and they're not known to be aggressive creatures, a cockatiel can bite and the bite may lead to minor and even severe injury. When these birds bite, they usually do so out of fear, not aggression. But since the danger of being bitten by a pet that possesses a sharp beak exists, it's not advisable for young children to own or handle cockatiels. Even the sweetest bird may react negatively from the tight grip of a small child who can't help but squeeze the cute bird.

- **Cage cleaning.** Just like all pet birds, cockatiels will leave droppings in their cage at all hours of the day. This means you, the pet owner, must have enough time each day cleaning its cage to keep your bird's living quarters germ-free. Cockatiels are also playful enough to toy with their food, spilling quite a few particles in the process. This means you'll have to clean up the cage in pretty much the same way a parent would a toddler's eating area. Make sure you have the time and patience to keep your pet's cage clean each day since a filthy cage can easily cause any animal to get sick.

- **The sounds they emit**. Cockatiels aren't known to learn human words as quickly as some parrot species—there are exceptions, of course, since every bird is different—but they can still be noisy little housemates. These pets can screech, whistle or mimic our sounds. Only get a pet cockatiel if you're fine with a pet that makes a bit of noise. Don't worry; it's not as loud and bothersome as a yelping puppy. Unless you have a neighbor with ultra-sensitive hearing, most cockatiels that are kept indoors won't be garnering you noise complaints.

Once you've taken these important points into consideration and you're convinced a pet cockatiel is right for you and your household, read on to discover more about these fascinating animals.

## 2.   Origin and Background

Cockatiels are known to hail from all over Australia, except in the region of Tasmania. They prefer to live in the eastern parts of the country, choosing dry inlands over coastal spots. The open environment provided by the Australian land mass is thought to be the reason why these birds don't possess the loud screeching sound of parrots, especially parrots that come from rainforest environments. This bird was initially discovered in 1770, but it didn't become a popular pet before the Australian gold rush occurred around the early 20th century. The initial sightings of cockatiels were reported by folks who arrived in Australia along with Captain Cook.

Cockatiels were once called Nymphicus in the early 1800s and were later taken to England and the rest of Europe, thanks to prevalent expeditions occurring during that century. While certain differences have been noted in the geographical populations, there are no subspecies of cockatiels.

Cockatiels in the wild search for food by flying close to the ground as they forage for their next meal. If you witness these birds in the wild, you may find them amongst a large flock of their own kind, circling the sky while looking for bodies of water. Lakes and the like offer cockatiels a place to breed, rest and seek refuge from the heat.

These birds have no trouble breeding in the wild and also breed with little difficulty in captivity, making them even more popular as pets. Their ease of breeding in captivity keeps the cost of purchasing a cockatiel fairly low.

In their natural habitat, cockatiels are frequently on high alert for predators. Because of this, they are light sleepers. It's not rare for a pet cockatiel to experience what's known as night-fright. A bird going through one of these episodes may thrash around its cage, acting very startled.

Tip: If you happen to have a pet cockatiel that experiences frequent night-frights, you can remedy the situation by leading it back to its perch stand and keeping a night light near the cage.

## 3.    Appearance of Cockatiels

Cockatiel breeders over the years have found ways to breed them in unique colors. Today, these birds come in many lovely color mutations, owning more colorful feathers than their original counterparts from decades and centuries ago.

You can now choose cockatiels in a wide array of hues. Some have gray feathers while others are colored yellow, soft brown, white and silver. There are a few select breeders with green mutations.

Furthermore, the markings of these creatures also vary. Some cockatiels have markings on different body parts while others come in solid colors, such as an all-white variety, or those with solid pearl hues. Plenty of cockatiels are made extra adorable thanks to orange, yellow, white, peach or gray cheek patches.

You may find cockatiels with unique appearances, like the cinnamon pearl pied whitefaces. These birds have mostly white feathers, plus a light cocoa brown shade around their wings. They may also have patches on their bodies. Some of these patches may appear in a lace-like pattern known as pearl markings. Female cockatiels that appear this way typically have light brown cheek patches while their male counterparts usually have all-white faces and no cheek patches.

Cockatiels possess an average length of approximately 14 inches and usually weigh anywhere from 75 to 120 grams, although it's not unusual for some well-fed pets to weigh as much as 200 grams.

Cockatiels or Nymphicus hollandicus originate from the Australian continent and they are also the members of the Cockatoo family. Cockatiels are considered small cockatoos and they are called Quarrion in Australia. Cockatiels were imported to Europe in 1840 and they were bred domestically in 1846 in France. Nowadays, they can be found all over the world, especially in the United States, where there are a larger number of cockatiel fanciers. In the wild, cockatiels are very noisy birds and live in large flocks, in arid inland areas, savannas, open woodlands, orchards, urban parks and farmlands.

Many wild cockatiels may be killed in some areas of Australia for the damages they produce to agriculture crops, but in other parts of this continent they are protected by law. These extraordinary birds mate for life. In the wild, cockatiels build their nest in tree hollows, as high as 5 feet above the ground. Cockatiels are considered the most widely kept and most popular parrots among other birds like budgerigars.

These birds migrate irregularly from place to place in search of water and food. They are also very good flyers.

There are several color mutations found in Cockatiels: Normal Gray, Lutino, Whiteface, Pearl, Platinum, Emerald, NSL Lutino, Ashenfallow, Dominant Silver, Parblue: Pastelface, Parblue: Creamface, Goldcheek, Dominant Yellowcheek, Fallow, Pale Fallow, Edged Dilute, Dilute, Faded, etc.

### Normal Gray Cockatiel
The Normal Gray cockatiel's plumage is dark grey with white wing bars, a yellow face and bright orange cheek patches.

### Lutino Cockatiel
The Lutino's plumage color can vary from light yellow to white. The male's, the female's and the youngsters' plumage coloration and the markings are the same. Their red eyes can vary from dark to bright red.

### Pearl Cockatiel
This bird has feathers on the nape, wings and back that are edged in yellow or white. The face is yellow with bright orange cheek patches. The male will lose most of his pearling by the second molt.

### Whiteface Cockatiel
Whiteface cockatiels' plumage color is mainly gray with the exception of the face, the head and the wings, which are white in color. The females present gray faces with some white streaks.

### Description
The Cockatiel is one of the smallest birds in the parrot family. Cockatiels are small parrots or crested cockatoos with a hooked bill and specific feet: two toes pointing forward and two pointing backward.

Wild cockatiels are mostly gray with a patch of white on the wings. The normal gray cockatiels are the original birds native to Australia. Males have a yellow head, yellow and grey crest and bright orange cheek patches, a small body and long pointed tail. Male cockatiels develop their yellow facial markings at about six months old. The females and youngsters are paler than the males. Females present only some spots of yellow color on their faces with orange ear coverts and a paler lower back. Young cockatiels develop their facial markings at six months.

The crest feathers of cockatiels is similar to cockatoos. They can move their crest feathers up and down when they are surprised, angry or sad. The eyes are dark brown, the beak is gray and the legs are grayish-brown in color. The cockatiel length is between 28-30 cm (11.02 -11.81 inches) from beak to the tip of the tail feathers, has an average wingspan of 35.56cm (14 inches) and weighs around 80-120 grams (0.17 - 0.26pounds).

### *Parts of a Cockatiel*
- Crest feathers
- Primary feathers
- Secondary feathers
- Crown
- Vent
- Mantle
- Leg
- Eye
- Tail
- Beak
- Throat
- Nape
- Ear coverts
- Band of wing

- Lesser wing coverts
- Secondary coverts
- Median wing coverts
- Scapulars
- Breast
- Abdomen
- Toe

# 4. Life span

In captivity, birds can live much longer than their wild relatives with the condition that they get all the necessary nutrition and care they need. Even in captivity, a lack of food, incomplete diet and improper care of parrots could lead to a considerably shorter life span. The cockatiel life span in the wild is 15-18 years and in captivity approximately 18-30 years.

# 5. The anatomy of cockatiels

The bird's body is covered with feathers, which helps maintain body temperature during flight. The feathers are made from keratin, the same protein found in our hair and nails. The feathers are covered with a thin layer of grease and feather powder. The grease is extracted with the help of the beak from the uropygial gland and distributed on the feathers. In some birds like pigeons and some species of parrots the uropygial gland is missing or is not properly developed and they have feather powder. A plumage that is permanently protected with grease or feather powder can't become wet, because the rain will just simply flow down from it.

There are several types of feathers:

- Contour feathers cover most of the surface of the bird and they protect the bird from sun, rain, wind and injury.

- Flight feathers are the large feathers of the wings and tail. The tail feathers act as brakes, controlling the orientation of flight. The flight feathers' bases are covered with smaller contour feathers called coverts. There are several layers of coverts on the wings.

- Down feathers are soft, fluffy and small feathers and can be found under the contour feathers.

- Filoplumes are very fine, hair-like feathers.

- Semiplumes provide aerodynamics, form and insulation.

- Bristle feathers are usually found on the head.

The skeleton of the bird is adapted to flight function, so the bones are hollow and lightweight, without marrow inside. In some bones, the hollow cavities contain an extension of the air sacs from the lungs, which helps the bird to get the oxygen it needs to fly easily and quickly.

The beak has no teeth, it's also known as bill and it has two parts: the upper mandible and the lower mandible. The upper mandible does not move independently from the skull and the lower mandible can move independently.

The wings of the bird are much like the arm and hand of a human. The more important muscles are the breast muscles and those of the wings.
The breast muscles represent one-third of the total body weight of the bird and they are attached to a large bone, called the keel. The keel extends from the breastbone (sternum) down along the chest and stomach.

Birds have a single nasal cavity and the larynx does not have vocal cords, it helps only to lock the trachea during swallowing. They have lungs and they also have nine air sacs through which air circulates. These air sacs allow a continuous flow of air through the respiratory system.

## 6.   Digestive components

The beak serves to pick up food and for seed peeling. The crop is the muscular pouch and it can be found at the end of the esophagus and serves as a chamber for storing and softening food, until the food already in the stomach moves on through the rest of the digestive system. The crop leads to a two-chambered stomach: one called proventriculus, which has the role of producing stomach enzymes for breaking down food, and the other chamber called ventriculus or gizzard, a powerful muscular organ, which takes the place of teeth and here the seeds and an assortment of grains of sand are squeezed until the seeds break up into a digestible form. From here, the food goes through thin then thick intestine and the digested food arrives in cloaca. The cloaca is the final part of a digestive tract and it is a small chamber with a mucous membrane. Parrots excrete their feces and their urine from the cloaca and it also plays an important role in reproduction.

The kidneys of the birds are located on both sides of the backbone and they are protected by the air sacs. Urine is eliminated through the cloaca and it can be a soft or solid substance and it contains uric acid, which makes it very corrosive.

Males have testicles and females have ovaries inside the body and when the birds are ready to breed, their reproductive organs (testes and ova) swell and produce the sperm and ova. The sperm is stored in the cloaca, until an opportunity to mate arises, and hens will receive the sperm into their cloaca before it will fertilize their ova.

Females have only one ovary and one oviduct, but in early stages of embryonic development each female bird has two ovaries and only the left ovary develops into a functional organ. During the breeding season the size of the ovary changes, becoming larger. Males have paired abdominal testes, which can be found inside of the cavity of the body. During breeding season the testes increase in size, becoming almost five times bigger than the initial size.

Most of the birds have their eyes placed on the side. With the help of their mobile neck, birds can see the surroundings in a radius of 360 degrees and can fly away rapidly if there is any danger nearby. The lower eyelid of the bird is mobile and the upper one is almost fixed. The third eyelid, which is called nictitating membrane, is hinged at the inner side of the eye and it serves to protect the eyes from bright light, wind, etc.

The ears are tiny, round holes situated on the right and left side of the head, behind the eyes and they are covered with feathers. There are no cartilaginous pavilions, but inside the ear there is the organ of balance. When the bird suffers from ear diseases, the organ of balance is also affected. A sick bird can't hold itself properly on the perches and its head is twisting to the affected ear.

## 7.    How to choose the right bird
### General criteria
Parrots are very lovely exotic birds, so if you want to be happy with your bird you have to study your parrot species personality and abilities. This will help to create a perfect pet-owner relationship, leading to a happy life together.

If you ask a few people who wish to have an exotic bird about what they are expecting from the bird, the answer will be: to be smart, to be beautiful, to be able to learn to speak as fast as possible, to have a perfect singing voice, to be a clean bird without damaging things in the house and the cost for everyday needs of the bird to be as cheap as possible. Before you make a decision to purchase a bird, you have to be aware of the fact that very few birds could match your expectations and you have to realize that these birds will be your companions for many years.

A parrot requires less time than a dog and it's easy to maintain, but don't forget that it will need food, cage cleaning and at least once a day fresh water. Your birds need your companionship and affection and it's very important to spend few moments a day with them.

If you are uncertain about keeping a pair or just a single parrot, then you have to take into consideration that a single bird is much easier to maintain and to train. If you don't have enough time to spend with him/her every single day, then I would strongly recommend buying a pair instead of a single bird.

If you decide to purchase a single bird, but you are uncertain about the bird's gender, then you have to take into consideration that the males are ideal pet birds and can be easier domesticated than females. Males are not as noisy and destructive as females during the breeding period and they can learn to speak much easier because of their capacity for imitation. Another piece of advice: take the bird with you if you are going in holiday if possible so that they can spend as much time as possible with you in the early days.

### How to purchase a healthy bird
Purchasing a bird directly from the breeder or from the pet store has multiple advantages. You can get information about their health conditions, their provenience and also you can check the quality of the environment where they've been kept. You have to know a few aspects which could indicate hidden diseases: the bird has to be active with a good stability on its feet; the nostrils must be clean without secretion; the feathers around the beak must be clean; the

bird's breathing has to be clear without whistling sounds; the eyes have to be clear; the missing feathers from the wings or tail could indicate "French molting"- viral disease which leads to feather loss; and dirty feathers (with feces) at the tail area could indicate digestive system problems.

### How to determine the parrot's gender

With some exceptions, parrots are sexually monomorphic, which means that their gender can't be determined by their markings or the color of their feathers. Differences of the appearance between the two genders are very small and you can't recognize the gender of the bird by looking at it. In cockatiels, some color mutations are monomorphic, but in Normal Grays, Fallows, Lutinos, Cinnamons and Silvers there are visual differences: males present bright orange cheek patches and bright yellow faces. The female will present paler cheek patches, a brown or gray face and paler barring on her tail feathers, etc.

The easiest and less expensive method for determining a parrot's gender is through quick DNA testing. There are lots of companies offering DNA testing as a mail-order service. You need some fresh cells of your bird so DNA can be extracted from them. You can get some cells of your bird by carefully plucking 2-4 feathers off the chest of the bird.

This is a little bit painful for the bird, but does not have any long-term effects. Feathers that are shed naturally are not suitable for extracting DNA (they lack blood and live cells). The pulled-out feathers can be sent to a specialized laboratory that offers sexing.

# 8.    All About Personality

### *Sociable Creatures*
Cockatiels are highly sociable creature, enjoying the company of both fellow cockatiels and their owners as well. A lonely cockatiel can act in a destructive manner, get depressed and may even fall physically ill. As long as they haven't been mistreated and have been handled by humans at a young age, cockatiels are sweet, docile and playful.

These birds aren't meant to be placed in a cage merely to be stared at or admired from afar. They love being talked to, played with and touched. Cockatiels will attempt to solicit attention by chirping, climbing on the cage bars, running back and forth, singing, displaying their feathers and exhibiting other attention-grabbing behavior. They may even begin to bang their toys and screech if they don't get the companionship they need. Show your pet cockatiel affection by rubbing its head, singing or talking to it and taking it out of it cage when it's ready. It's not unusual for these birds to reciprocate your touches by preening your eyebrows, for instance, or giving you gentle pecks with its beak.

Since they're sociable birds even in the wild, cockatiels enjoy eating with the other members of the family, and this includes their human family. Try to include your cockatiel into as many activities at home, as long as it's safe to do so (never leave them alone unattended with young children or other pets like dogs and cats). Have your bird by your side as you surf the Internet, let it perch on your shoulders while you watch your favorite TV show, or enjoy snacking together.

### *Intelligent Pets*

Cockatiels are intelligent birds. While their intelligence is an attractive trait that makes them extra fun and interesting, being smart also means cockatiels need plenty of mental stimulation from their environment and you, their handler. Unhappy birds may exhibit behaviors like nibbling and plucking out their own feathers, even to the point of being stripped bare.

When cockatiels are ignored for too long or too regularly, they are prone to loneliness and depression. And what happens when this bird gets too depressed? It can go as far as refusing to eat and dying from starvation. That's how much company and mental stimulation means to a cockatiel.

As a responsible owner, it's important to keep bird toys in your cockatiel's cage. Pick colorful toys, as these attract the bird more than plain looking ones, but do experiment since every bird is unique.

**Tip:** Be sure to leave a variety of toys but allow your pet to play with only bird-safe toys. Toys meant for other animals, such as cats, may be inappropriate and dangerous for your cockatiel. Check your pet's toys for signs of wear and tear. Discard any broken toy to keep your cockatiel from harm.

These birds typically enjoy toys they can shred apart or chewed on. Other great choices are bird toys they can throw around with their beaks, or pull apart.

**Tip:** To keep things interesting for your cockatiel, rotate its toys every week. Bring out a group of toys for one week then hide them before taking out a second group of toys for the following week.

Since they're intelligent creatures, cockatiels enjoy exploring. A fun activity for your pet is exploring different rooms inside your home. These birds tend to use their beaks while exploring, especially when examining new objects. Expect a cockatiel to chew often. They'll chew on wood, paper, plastic, cloth, rubber, metal and anything else that catches their fancy. Since chewing is an instinctive behavior for them, you will have to watch over your bird when it's exploring areas outside the cage.
Note: Common items that can prove dangerous for your bird when it chews on them include electric wires, plants, rusty metals, moldy food and anything that contains lead.

### *Entertaining Companion*
As long as you keep a cockatiel happy by providing it plenty of mental stimulation and company, expect these creatures to be entertaining. Even simple acts like watching your pet bird eat, wash itself, preen and play with toys can be very fun for you.

Many cockatiels can be taught tricks like ringing a bell on command, pulling specific toys, and walking up ladders. Being a member of the parrot family, cockatiels may be taught to mimic human words, although keep in mind these birds aren't the fastest learners of speech, especially when compared to other types of parrots like the African Gray. Cockatiels may also learn to sing and mimic non-human sounds, like the ringing of your home telephone. Do expect the sound of a cockatiel to come off as more muffled and unclear than those emitted by larger parrots.

The talking ability of cockatiels is linked to the male hormone testosterone. Because of this correlation between bird-speak and testosterone, male cockatiels are more likely to talk and mimic sounds than their female counterparts. While some females do learn to talk, the chances of a male cockatiel speaking are significantly higher. And what does a talking cockatiel sound like? These birds usually prefer to use a feminine, high-pitched voice.

Expect your pet cockatiel to be quite vocal, especially as soon as they arise in the morning, or when they're about to go to sleep at night. Being sociable creatures, they like saying "good morning" and "good night" to their flock, meaning you and anyone else who lives in the same house.
Cockatiels will be extra noisy if you leave them alone for a while. As soon as you come home, your pet will most likely greet you loudly. It's their way of communicating, as if they're letting you know how happy they are to see you return.

Can these birds be demanding? You bet. Like pet dogs or cats, cockatiels can learn to be spoiled and figure out quite quickly how they can get you to do what they want. When this happens and you have a spoiled cockatiel in your hands, excessive screaming can occur—from your bird and perhaps even you!

Don't end up frustrated as a pet owner with a cockatiel who misbehaves. For example, if your cockatiel screams and you come running to their cage to see what it wants, this tells your bird that screaming is effective and will continue to exhibit screeching behavior to get you to come closer each time. The bird will start to think that screaming acts like a "remote control". To keep this from happening, don't give in to your bird's demands when it screams or does other unattractive things like banging its toys loudly to get attention.

While it can be a challenge to keep a pet cockatiel from being loud, it's not an impossible feat. Just like owning any intelligent pet, you'll need to exhibit patience and dedicate time. Cockatiels are very much conditioned to love routines and repetitive tasks. Similar to a human baby learning swiftly how crying gets mommy to come to his crib and give him what he wants, a cockatiel will try whatever gets results.

Do introduce your pet cockatiels to healthy routines. If he squawks all the time for attention, don't come running. These birds can be very persistent at times. Some will wear out their owner's patience by simply getting louder and louder until their human gives in. When you're pretty certain your pet is being noisy simply for attention and not because it's ill, get busy doing something else while ignoring the cockatiel.

The whole point is you want to tell your cockatiel that throwing a loud tantrum won't give it what it wants. Perhaps you can go for a walk or relax in front of the TV. This communicates to your pet that you will not surrender to its demands when it acts spoiled and loud.

**Tip**: Be patient. If your cockatiel is used to you running to do its bidding after a crying spell, it might take several repetitions before your bird adjusts to your new routine of ignoring the crying.

### *Potential for Fright*
Cockatiels experience feelings of fright just like any other pet. The things that alarm these birds the most include loud noises and voices, and also sudden movements. When they're frightened, these birds may react aggressively. They tend to bite, hiss or scream. Some birds may turn away instead, and turn its back towards you or any other source of its fear. It's also not rare to find a scared cockatiel hiding at the bottom part of a cage.
Because we can't avoid certain things that scare these birds such as loud noises, it's advisable to provide your pet places where it can hide in its cage. One way to do this is to have a cage with corners so

your cockatiel can hide in one of the corners whenever it feels threatened. Another thing you can do is to tuck the cage in a place far from noise. You can try placing your cockatiel's cage up against a wall, away from hallways, doors, windows and the TV.

As mentioned earlier, cockatiels are prone to experience what's called "night-frights". These frights typically occur when something awakens the bird while it's sleeping at night, causing it to feel extremely startled. A bird going through one of these episodes will typically start to flap its wings rapidly in an effort to fly away from whatever is causing it fear.

There is the potential for danger when night-frights take place because your pet cockatiel can end up with a damaged wing. It can hit anything - be it cage bars, toys and other objects - while the bird is vigorously flapping its wings out of fright. One way to help avoid night-frights is leaving a soft nightlight near your pet's cage. Turn this light on each day as soon as it gets dark in the room.

### *Sources of Stress*

Aside from loud noises, there are other sources of stress for cockatiels. These are moody birds that generally dislike change. They love routine, probably because routine means security.

Even minor changes like changing the color of the curtains in the room where your cockatiel lives can stress it out. Many pet owners notice their cockatiels get stressed when the owner wears new cologne. Some cockatiels dislike strangers so much they will screech when an unfamiliar person visits. The birds may act aggressively even after the visitor leaves. These pets also don't like it when you change routines at home.

When cockatiels are stressed, their immune system gets compromised, increasing the risk of getting physically ill through infections and other diseases. Furthermore, unhealthy, malnourished and stressed out pet birds can get sick if their cage is located in a drafty area. Spots with moving air tend to provide these birds with an environment with constantly changing temperatures, plus varying temperatures in different areas of the cage.

Most birds are unable to withstand a temperature drop of 10 or more degrees Fahrenheit within a 24-hour period. A cockatiel experiencing rapid temperature drops can get very sick. Keeping your pet bird well nourished and stress-free makes them less prone to getting ill from drafts. But even a mostly healthy bird may experience stress without you being aware, so it's always best to keep birdcages away from drafty spots in your home.

**Tip**: How do you know if a spot has draft? Hold a candle and light it in the area. If you see the flame flickering then chances are good it's a drafty spot, definitely not a good choice for your cockatiel's cage location.

## 9.    Females Versus Males

Should you get a male or female pet? Is there a difference between the personalities of a typical male cockatiel and that of a female? Generally, yes, although there are exceptions. Remember, no two birds are completely alike in temperament, and this is especially true for an intelligent and sociable creature like the cockatiel.

Females tend to act more nervous than their male counterparts, but they also have a higher chance of being friendlier and more affectionate than males. It's more difficult to teach a female how to talk but they do chirp in a charmingly friendly and singsong way.

Male cockatiels have bigger bodies than females and, like the majority of bird species, often have brighter and more colorful feathers than the females. Males can act more aggressive than females and the likelihood of being bitten is higher with a male cockatiel over a female one. There is also more exhibition of typical hormonal aggressive behavior from the boys even when no female is in sight.

The good news about male cockatiels is they do sing and talk more. They're surprisingly better at parenting than the females. While the mommy cockatiels are in charge of hatching the eggs and caring for their newborns, the males don't leave and abandon the babies. When experiencing fatherhood, male cockatiels become very protective of their young, especially in the wild where predators abound. The males can be considered nurturing and warm towards their offspring. In situations where the mother cockatiel is injured or killed, the father typically steps in and fulfills its role as a parent capably and willingly.

An important thing you must know if you choose a female cockatiel is that, even without a mate, they are prone to laying unfertilized eggs. These eggs don't house a baby cockatiel and will never hatch. This can pose a risk to your pet's health.

If she ends up egg-bound, your cockatiel may need emergency medical attention from an avian vet. If she lays egg chronically, you will need to bring her to a vet as well.

## 10. Dusty Animals

Cockatiels produce plenty of dust, otherwise known as powder down. The birds produce the down naturally. Compared to many other bird species, a cockatiel's body has plenty of down, making them one of the dustiest pet birds to own.

Expect to find white powder all over your pet's living quarters - this includes their cage and any object situated near the cage. When a cockatiel shakes out its feathers, you'll see a cloud of the dusty down. Don't be surprised to see a coating of white powder on your skin after you've pet your cockatiel. If you have allergies or asthma, find out beforehand if a cockatiel is something you can own. Handle someone's pet cockatiel before making a commitment to owning one.

Even though misty baths can get rid of some of the bird's down, it's practically impossible to get rid of all of the powder. Anyone allergic to the down is better off with a different type of pet. If asthma or allergies are present in you or someone in your household, it's best to speak with a doctor before bringing any bird home.

## 11.   Costs of Owning a Cockatiel

The cost of owning a small bird as a pet can quickly add up. The total price tag can be more than what you initially expected. Don't acquire a pet cockatiel under the false assumption that it will cost less than a cat or a dog. Don't assume it will take up less of your time than other pets. A cockatiel will need a bigger cage than a canary or other smaller pet birds. It will also require more handling and bonding time than plenty of other pets like a fish or a turtle. These birds will need a steady supply of food, durable toys and some basic training.

Some of the beginner items you'll need for a pet cockatiel are listed below (For more details, read the chapter Supplies and Accessories):
- Bird cage $100/ £77
- Bag of bird food $20/ £16
- Several toys $10/ £7.70
- Food and water bowls $15/ £12
- Swing $5/ £4
- Ladder $7 /£5.60
- Perches $4 /£3.20
- Bird bath $70/ £56
- Nail clipper $6/ £4.50
- Travel carrier $45/ £36

Even a relatively inexpensive bird like a cockatiel will need a financial commitment from you. Keep in mind, too, the additional expenses you will incur during your bird's life. These will include tests at the vet's office, such as tests for psittacosis, and vaccinations and perhaps micro-chipping. Other expenses you must expect to pay for throughout owning a pet cockatiel are bird seeds and pellets, treats, fruits and vegetables, vitamin supplements, cage and bird cleaning supplies, toys and routine exams at the vet. Your cockatiel will typically need vaccinations and wing-clippings.

Before deciding to bring a cockatiel into your home for yourself and the rest of your family, make a careful decision to figure out if you can afford one, both financially and time-wise. Don't make an impulse buy, only to be unable to provide the kind of environment that will keep you and the bird happy and healthy. All types of pets need a certain degree of time and money.

## 12.   A Cockatiel and the Rest of the Family

It's smarter to acquire a pet cockatiel for an entire family, as opposed to buying one for a child. Families with children aged 5 years or less are better off waiting until the children are a little bit older before bringing home a cockatiel. These birds can be very moody and will react negatively towards loud noises and sudden movements, elements that younger children are sure to provide. Chances are, the energetic movements and voices of toddlers will provide stress rather than a positive experience for most cockatiels.

Compared to many other parrots, cockatiels have small beaks but they can still deliver a mean bite. Their bites can break skin and cause bleeding. It's not rare for a cockatiel to clamp down with their beaks, refusing to release the bite. When it feels threatened, a cockatiel's bite can stay on like a hard grip for several seconds.

Cockatiels can make wonderful pets for older children who understand and know how to handle the animal gently and respectfully. These birds can be tamed with ease. They enjoy spending time with humans outside of the cage habitat. They don't just tolerate human attention; they crave and enjoy our company immensely.

These birds have the tendency to become one-person pets if they don't get used to being handled by other members of the family. The more people at home play with the cockatiel, the better. Thanks to social activities from different people, your bird will less likely bite or act aggressively out of fear.

If you have responsible older children, the daily care a cockatiel needs can be accomplished by the whole family. The children can take care of washing the bird's bowls, cleaning the cage and providing bird feeds. No matter what age your children are, always provide parental supervision and monitor your children as they fulfill their pet owner duties. Accomplishing these chores together will bring you closer as a family and help everyone bond with your charming pet.

# Chapter 2. Supplies and Accessories

In the first chapter, we discussed how cockatiels can be one of the most affectionate and entertaining pets around. Small, very intelligent and sociable, a happy bird will bring hours of entertainment and companionship to the right owner and household.

The bird's warm and engaging personality makes it very trainable. It's no wonder cockatiels are some of the most popular pet birds. When cared for properly by the right handler, these birds are fascinating and unforgettable.

Inexperienced bird owners who are willing to invest time learning about these birds can own a pet cockatiel. The vital thing is that you're aware of its needs, including its keen need to socialize. Since cockatiels have natural playful and friendly personalities, they will only thrive with an owner who's able to spend time with them.

Other than a cockatiel's desire to bond with other family members, just like any pet, it has specific needs in terms of food, housing, bedding, health and fun. This chapter will cover the supplies you the pet owner will have to provide your bird.

From details on the right cage size for your feathery friend to the type of food it requires to lead a healthy and long life, in this section you'll learn what to prepare at home before welcoming a cockatiel. The goal is to be prepared as early as possible so you and your cockatiel will get to spend several happy years together.

# 1.  Cage Requirements

The first thing you're going to need before you bring home your pet cockatiel is a cage that has enough room for your new housemate. Generally speaking, these birds are most comfortable in the type of cage they're used to. If you're acquiring your bird from a previous owner directly, ask for the cage the cockatiel already lived in. This will lessen the stress from the move.

**Tip**: If the previous cage is too small, you should upgrade it to one with a more suitable size (which we will discuss in a moment) but during your bird's first few days adjusting to your home, it helps to house it in the enclosure the bird's used to.

Young cockatiels are good at adapting. Eventually they'll grow to like any cage after an adjustment period. Fortunately, when it comes to enclosures, there are a few options that are suitable for these birds. You can choose to place your cockatiel outside or inside your house. Pre-made versions of either kind of dwellings may be purchased. The ideal temperature is 70 to 80 degrees Fahrenheit. They can tolerate higher and lower, but those are comfortable range medians. If you live in a considerably warmer or colder area, you may want to keep them indoors or possibly indoors depending on the season.

Another option is building your new pet's living quarters in a room indoors, or from an alcove. Big store-bought, powder-coated cages meant for parrots are also excellent choices. Cages you can find for sale can range from very simple wire cages to fancy looking varieties. When it comes to narrowing down your choices, think about some factors to help you find the best match.

## *Comfort*

Expect your new pet to explore and perch at the top portion of any type of cage you provide. Because of this natural cockatiel tendency, it's best to go with long cages rather than tall ones. In the eyes of these birds, it's the length of the cage that matters. The longer the cage, the roomier it will feel for a cockatiel.

It's typical for cockatiels to spend most of its hours enclosed at the top portion of the cage. Don't choose a cage shorter than two feet in length. Your bird will be happier and healthier when it has sufficient room for fun and exercise.

### Bar Spacing
Cockatiels are very inquisitive little creatures. They love to explore and tinker with objects. This means choosing the wrong kind of cage can be dangerous for your bird. Cockatiels are prone to being curious about the other side of the cage bars. They seem to always be itching to go out and play with something located just outside their enclosure. Because of this, choose a cage with bar spacing that is close together; close enough so your pet won't be able to get its head through the bars.

**Tip**: As a rule, cages with bars that are half an inch to three-quarters of an inch apart are ideal choices.

Always check for the material of the cage bars. Look to see if they're made of safe materials. A simple aviary wire does the job of housing a bird well but if your cockatiel were to chew on the wire, it could get zinc poisoning. To prevent this from happening, always wash new cages or wires using a vinegar solution before housing any bird inside.
It's vital to check the materials of any enclosure you prepare for your cockatiel since poisoning is always a possibility. Zinc poisoning is a type of heavy metal poisoning. Vets can give emergency medical attention to birds experiencing zinc or lead poisoning. Instead of relying on emergency care, however, it's best to remember the adage

"an ounce of prevention is better than a pound of cure". Make an effort not to expose your pet to risky cage materials.

Be on the lookout for cast-iron cages. Some of these are welded with lead solder, a dangerous material for your bird. Cockatiels love to chew or nibble on just about anything around them and chewing on cast-iron wires may lead to heavy metal poisoning.

**Tip**: How will you know if a cage is lead-free? Use a lead test kit, one typically used to check items for child-safety.

The majority of big cast iron cages are made with a durable industrial finish known as powder coating. There have been reports of this type of cage containing zinc. When your pet ends up chewing off the coating of these enclosures, poisoning can follow.

Unfortunately, unlike lead tests, home tests for zinc aren't something you can buy. To find out about zinc content on a particular cage you're interested in, get in touch with the cage's manufacturer and inquire about the paint used on the item. If you already own a cage and are worried it contains zinc, you have the option of sending samples to a lab for safety testing.

### Cleaning

If you want to make your life easier as a pet bird owner in the long haul, consider the amount of cleaning a potential enclosure will require. Cages shaped like rectangles are generally easier to clean than round ones. Round cages make folding newspapers to line the bottom extra difficult. If possible, select a cage that comes with a grate. The grate keeps the bird away from fallen food and droppings. Having a deep tray located beneath the grate makes daily cleaning tasks far less arduous.

You might have noticed cages that come with shields that extend out from the cage. The good thing about these shields is how they keep your cockatiel's droppings away from the floor. On the flipside, the droppings end up on the shield that will need to be cleaned often.

Choose a cage with a big door so reaching into the cage for whatever reason is as easy as possible. The best cages allow you to reach every nook inside through the door. If you're going for some of the bigger cages, keep in mind that the only way to completely clean the larger ones is with a hose.

### More about the cage door
We can't stress enough how it'll make your life much easier if you go with a cockatiel cage that has a large front door. Compared to other small birds, cockatiels are quite large. A cage with a small door meant for a parakeet isn't a good choice for a cockatiel.

Whenever anyone needs to reach inside the cage, especially during the daily cleaning required, you will see how a roomy cage definitely makes the task easier. It's wonderful to have enough space to maneuver your hand around the cage, thanks to a big cage door. You'll also find cages that come with doors that convert to perches, making it unnecessary to purchase additional cage-top perch equipment.

Having extra openings in an enclosure can also help. This is especially true if you plan on breeding cockatiels in the future. Choosing a cage equipped with an opening located high in the cage is excellent because you can attach a nesting box there. Without a pre-built opening, you'll have to cut a hole in the cage in order to attach the nesting box, giving you extra work and the possibility of a ruined cage.

## Food and water in the cage

Keep your cockatiel's water and food bowls in a spot inside the cage that is easily accessible from outside. It's a great idea to have a minimum of three bowls for your bird: one for water, the second bowl for feed and a third bowl for vegetables.

**Tip**: You can add a fourth bowl for treats if you wish. You'll find the majority of parrot cages are sold with only two bowls. Purchase an additional one, plus treat cups.

## Safety in mind

Always make safety your number one priority when choosing your cockatiel's cage. No matter how pretty some ornaments look, if they aren't made to be safe toys for cockatiels, it's best to skip them, as they can be dangerous for your bird.

These energetic and playful pets can wedge a wing in tight places. Steer clear of round cages designed with wire bars, especially when the bars narrow in some places. This type of enclosure is extra dangerous for birds, as the creature can get a foot or a wing stuck in any narrow opening. When making the final decision regarding your cockatiel's enclosure, look at the housing from the eyes of a curious bird. Imagine the potential trouble your pet can get into while inside its living quarters. Go for the enclosure that poses the least number of risks.

## Cage Location

Think of the cage as your bird's universe. This is the spot where the cockatiel will spend the majority of its time. The cage protects and shields your pet, as well as protects your own things from the inquisitive nature of the cockatiel. With its curious tendencies to explore, plus its sharp beak, these birds can destroy furniture or décor in a quick minute.

When choosing where to place your cockatiel's cage, pick a spot where the bird can be close to where plenty of family activities occur. Don't put the cage right in the middle of any hustle and bustle, however. While cockatiels are very sociable, loud noises and sudden movements stress them out.

Cockatiels are known to get very comfortable living in cages placed against a wall. This way it can watch activities going on inside the room and not feel insecure, worried that someone might sneak up behind the cage.

Another factor to consider is the amount of irregular activities occurring in a location. Don't place your cockatiel's cage in places where they may easily feel surprised. This includes areas with blind spots. A person suddenly coming into view can startle your bird.

When it comes to windows, don't place your bird's cage near a spot that gets too much natural heat from the sun. You don't want the sun overheating your pet. It's a good idea to place the cage close to a window if you want to keep your bird entertained. Birds will enjoy watching activities taking place outside.

The kitchen is a terrible choice for any birdcage. There is a huge risk your cockatiel will breathe in poisonous fumes. The smoke emitted from non-stick cookware, for instance, can act like a high dose of air pollution to any bird. Place the cage in a spot where you and the rest of the members of your household like to hang out.

Keep the bottom part of the cage lined with newspaper or some other safe product. After doing so to a clean cage, the cage is now ready to be called home.

## 2.    Housing Supplies

After you have found a suitable cage for your cockatiel, the next step is to provide other supplies. Your new friend is going to need more than a roof over its head in order to thrive.

Here are the basic housing supplies to keep your cockatiel happy, healthy and as stress-free as possible.

### *Toys*

Cockatiels certainly enjoy chewing. Giving your bird access to bird-friendly toys will keep them happy. Chewing and being curious are natural tendencies in these creatures and proving them an outlet for these inclinations will help keep their stress levels down. Bored cockatiels tend to act out. They may pick their own feathers when highly stressed. Only purchase toys that are marked safe for cockatiels. Your pet may quickly choke from playing with an inappropriate toy. Bird toys made with palm strips, twig balls and natural vegetable-tanned leather materials are excellent choices. Cockatiels, like larger birds, also enjoy wooden toys. Do make sure not to choose one that is made for a much larger bird species. Your cockatiel might not be able to chew on a toy that's too big. Cheap and safe toy options include brand new popsicle sticks and balsa wood. Balled up paper works as a homemade toy, too.

Check your pet's toys and accessories often, as frequently as every day. Any worn or damaged toy should be thrown away as these can cause injury to your cockatiel. It's a great habit to rotate your bird's toys, as it's normal for these creatures to find their toys boring after a period. When your pet isn't paying a toy any more attention, hide it for a few days and place different toys to take the previous toy's place. Avoid putting an unfamiliar toy inside a cockatiel's dwelling place without doing an initial introduction. Try to introduce new items in a neutral location so your bird won't feel stressed out in its own cage, thanks to a new and strange item in its eyes. If you have a new toy for your cockatiel, place it for a few days just outside the birdcage. Give your pet enough time to get used to the new toys and accessories.

Many cockatiel owners think mirrors are good toys for their birds. On the contrary, mirrors don't make appropriate toys because these creatures are prone to bond with their own reflections. Birds see their own image as another bird. This is especially true for cockatiels kept alone. You, the owner, will have a more challenging time bonding with and training your pet if a mirror is provided. Two or more cockatiels kept in the same cage won't need a mirror at all because they have each other for company and games.

### *Perches*
The type of perches you provide your cockatiel will matter a lot. Imagine being on your feet all hours of the day, just like this bird. Wouldn't you want to stand on the most comfortable surface possible? The kind of perches in the cage plays a huge role in the comfort and health of your pet. Cockatiels require different types of sizes and textures when it comes to their perches. The right perches will give your pet the proper kind of exercise for its feet. For an animal that spends all of its years on its toes, so to speak, the health of their legs are of utmost importance.

You'll find plenty of bird perches available on the market. They come in varieties like durable plastic, wood, rope and concrete. Some perches even resemble ladders to make things extra interesting for the birds. Some perches are designed to go straight across, while others are built to go diagonally. The different directions provide various ways for the cockatiel to climb, keeping it active and entertained.

Give your pet access to natural branches. A terrific example is a Manzanita perch since this will give your pet different widths to rest on. The varying width makes it easy for your pet to exercise its feet. In the wild, most branches aren't built in perfectly straight lines. Try to emulate the natural perches by providing branches as perches.

Before you grab any branch outdoors to use as a perch for your cockatiel, keep in mind some random branch pulled out of your neighborhood may contain all kinds of pesticides that are used to treat trees. Make sure your source for a natural branch is a pesticide-free tree. Clean any branch thoroughly. Never add a natural branch without washing it prior to putting it inside your cockatiel's home. To clean natural tree branches, cut each branch to a size suitable for your pet's cage. Scrub to clean the branch, washing it in a solution made of 10 parts water and one part bleach. Rinse the new perch thoroughly with water. Next, set your oven to 200 degrees Fahrenheit and heat any branch for 45 minutes.

You may also use a perch to dull your cockatiel's nails, saving you some grooming time. Look for a bird-grooming perch. These are typically made of concrete. You'll also find a variety that has a sand blasted finish. Don't provide any more than one bird-grooming perch per cage. You don't want your cockatiel's feet to always be perched on an abrasive material.

The only way to find out if your bird will like a particular perch is by testing the perch out with the cockatiel. In terms of size, a good size for a perch is one where the toes of your bird wrap ½ to ¾ inches of the way around. It should have a diameter of one to one and a half inches.

**Tip**: If you find your pet's toes touch around the perch, this means the perch's diameter is too small. If, however, the bird's toes lie flat on its perch, this means the perch is way too wide.

## *Lighting*

As many new cockatiel owners experience, the middle of the night can bring in some frightening sounds. If you're unaware or new to the common cockatiel phenomenon known as "night-frights" then you just might be as frightened as your pet. Night-frights are very common among these birds. The cockatiel may start to thrash around and often screech loudly when these episodes occur.

In most cases, something in the dark alarmed the bird and caused it to experience a night-fright. The trigger can be a shadow or a noise. In an effort to protect itself, a cockatiel will attempt to take off in flight, only to end up thrashing around its cage out of panic. Plenty of cockatiels sustain injuries due to thrashing about from night-frights.

To reduce night-frights, place a nightlight close to your cockatiel's cage. See how your bird reacts to the light and allow it several nights to get used to the change. Since each bird is different, your pet may require a longer duration to feel less stressed at night. If you find your cockatiel hasn't adjusted to the nightlight after a week and the night-frights haven't disappeared, perhaps your pet might prefer its cage to be covered in complete darkness. See what works and adjust the lighting situation for your cockatiel according to its personal reaction.

If the lighting adjustments don't reduce the cockatiel's night-frights, you will have to do some evaluation and figure out your pet's personal preferences. See if you can find and then eliminate the source of the frights. It can be a cat stalking your pet, bright headlights that flash a window at night, or it might be a certain sound that occurs only in the evening.

**Tip**: If your pet continues to thrash at night, you might want to consider setting up another cage just for nighttime use-one without toys or perches to lessen the injury the cockatiel might sustain from acting in panic. Line the cage with towels for extra cushion and protection.

As for the type of light to have during your cockatiel's waking hours, a full-spectrum light situated above its cage is a great source of Vitamin D. Incandescent, full-spectrum bulbs are good choices and work well if you have free space for a lamp right next to your pet's cage. Many types of windows unfortunately filter out natural Vitamin D from the sun, making additional lights necessary. When installing lighting fixtures, keep cords out of your bird's reach. Remember birds require approximately 10 to 12 hours of rest daily.

## 3.    Food and Nutrition

The most crucial thing to remember when you're planning a cockatiel's diet is variety. When it comes to food, these wonderful creatures are smart and sociable enough to let you know what it likes, what it hates and what it simply can't get enough of.

Don't ever force a cockatiel to eat food it doesn't enjoy. Leave it to your pet to choose what it will eat. If your bird eats just a tiny portion of any other type of food besides its usual seeds and pellets, that's normal as well. The important thing, after all, is the presence of variety in your pet's diet.

### Eating Habits

When these birds consume table foods, they end up eating fewer pellets. Birds are prone to eating as much food as their bodies need and nothing more. Cockatiels eat about 15 grams of high-energy food each day. Your goal as the pet owner is to feed your bird 15 grams of nutrient-rich food daily.

Aside from pellets, give your cockatiel a wide array of healthy foods each day so it gets to eat a balanced and healthy diet. Learn about the

41

toxic foods you should never serve your cockatiel. These can make your pet sick and even lead to death.

### Toxic Foods
*The following are the most commonly found toxic foods for cockatiels* (bear in mind this isn't a complete list. There may be other common household items not listed here that can harm your pet, if in doubt don't feed it and talk with a vet):

- Rhubarb
- Avocados
- Potato leaves and stems
- Tomato
- Alcohol
- Eggplant
- Coffee
- Tea
- Bean plants
- Chocolate
- Salt
- Sugar
- Oily foods
- Fruit seeds or pits (especially those from apricots, apples, oranges, peaches, cherries, plums and pears)
- Tobacco
- Don't feed cockatiels shellfish like crab, shrimp or lobster. These contain high amounts of bacterial contamination. Common bacteria found in shellfish are generally safe for us to eat but may prove toxic to birds.

### Fruit and Vegetables
When giving your pet veggies and fruit, make the portions small and, whenever possible, serve the produce shredded, chopped or cut

into tiny pieces. The small size will motivate most cockatiels to grab and try a wide array of fruits and vegetables.

When serving produce, thoroughly wash every veggie and fruit before offering any to your pet. You want to make sure none of its food contains pesticides and other harmful chemicals.

**Tip**: To clean fruit and vegetables properly, soak them in a bowl of cold water. Allow the produce to soak for a few minutes. Afterwards, rinse off with fresh water before giving them to your cockatiel.

Certain vegetables are not toxic to cockatiels but they provide very low amounts of vitamins and minerals. Examples of such nutritionally poor veggies are celery, iceberg lettuce and cucumbers. These are mainly comprised of water and don't contain many nutrients. If your pet happens to love these water-rich varieties, provide them as occasional treats.
When choosing the most nutrient-dense vegetables, go for those with vibrant orange hues, as well as dark green vegetables. These contain the most amount of vitamins.

Certain vegetables are best served moderately, once or twice each week and no more. Varieties like spinach and parsley have oxalic acid, a type of acid that binds with calcium. Consuming these veggies can lead to less calcium being absorbed in the bird's body, stressing out the kidneys. Serving your pet a diet rich in oxalic acid may lead to poor blood clotting and even convulsions. Even low amounts of oxalates can cause decreased growth, poor bone health and painful kidney stones.

While you don't have to completely eliminate all produce containing oxalic acid from your cockatiel's diet, remember to serve them no more than two times in a week. Other veggies containing oxalic acid—although in smaller amounts—are carrots, beet greens, collard greens, turnips, berries and lettuce.

Veggies like broccoli have phytate or phytic acid. These phytates can cause the same side effects as oxalic acid, leading to decreased calcium absorption in the cockatiel. The absorption of essential zinc and iron is known to also decrease in the process, depriving your bird of these necessary nutrients.

Many green vegetables are comprised of large amounts of water, some made of 90 percent water. Serving too many green vegetables per day can lead to excess urine in the cockatiel. Traces of phytates can be found in legumes, broccoli, carrots, nuts, potatoes, carrots, green beans, berries and sweet potatoes. Always serve these in moderation, no more than two times a week.

Plenty of sugar can be found in carrots and sweet potatoes. A diet rich in sugar can lead to yeast infections in the bird. You can serve these foods as occasional treats. If you decide to give your cockatiel grapes or strawberries, remember these fruits rot swiftly. Discard any discolored, bruised or mushy produce right away, keeping your bird's home clean and free from fungal and bacterial infections.

When attempting to serve a cockatiel a balanced diet with variety, keep in mind which foods should only be served once or twice weekly. Every day, provide a fresh supply of fruit and vegetables to your bird. Try not to serve the same type of food each day.

Because plenty of fruits and veggies that cockatiels love are sources of an enzyme inhibitor or a natural toxin such as those mentioned above, it's crucial to aim for variety in the pet's diet. Serving a wide array of food ensures your cockatiel gets all kinds of nutrients. A selection of fresh foods daily will provide your bird the best nutritional sources.

Great choices of vegetables are:

- Spinach
- Sprouts
- Turnip Greens
- Mustard Greens
- Swiss chard
- Chicory
- Broccoli
- Escarole
- Tomatoes
- Bok Choi
- Beet Greens
- Collard greens
- Grated Carrots
- Corn on the Cob
- Kale
- Endive
- Yams
- Sweet potato
- Pumpkin.

Cockatiels love the following fruits:

- Mangos
- Apples
- Nectarines
- Apricots
- Papayas
- Bananas
- Peaches
- Grapes
- Oranges
- Cantaloupe.

Note: Never give your cockatiel fruits with seeds because some seeds can be highly toxic. One example is the pits of cherries. These have trace amounts of cyanide.

### Pellets or Seeds?

While many people like to argue and pick sides in choosing between either pellets or seeds as the best food for cockatiels, a good reminder is that balance and variety in your cockatiel's diet is key. Provided your pet is getting a variety of foods, there is no need to feed it just either pellets or seeds. You can feed both to your bird.

If you feed your cockatiel seeds, always keep the seed tray clean. Wash the tray with hot, soapy water to keep it from growing fungus and bacteria. Before serving seeds, make sure the seed tray is totally dry. The presence of moisture on a seed tray provides a healthy breeding ground for harmful fungus and bacteria, something you and your bird won't be very happy about.

Cockatiels like to get seeds from the husks. Because of this feeding habit, you are likely to find the bird's bowl filled with empty husks that your pet didn't eat. Be on the lookout for rotting or discarded food and keep the seed tray clean and filled with fresh seeds.

When purchasing a bag of seeds at any pet store, place the seeds in your freezer when you get home to keep them fresh and bug-free. Keep the seeds in a sealed or re-sealable bag so moisture doesn't enter. By keeping your seeds in the freezer, they will remain fresh for several months.

### Water

A cockatiel's water source must be kept clean. Change the water bowl every day, plus any time the water becomes dirty. Food and bird droppings may fall into the water bowl. Keep water trays washed and cleaned using hot soapy water. This helps keep bacteria and fungus from growing and infecting your bird.

## *Protein*
Is it fine to feed cockatiels meat? Yes, as long as your pet only eats tiny amounts. Cockatiels can eat very limited servings of beef, chicken or fish. Another excellent source of protein for your bird is cooked chicken eggs. You can serve them scrambled or hard-boiled. See if your bird enjoys yogurt or cottage cheese - other wonderful sources of protein.

When serving your cockatiel meat or eggs, it's advisable to serve only freshly cooked meat and eggs. Avoid giving your pet fish, eggs or meat that have already been refrigerated then re-heated. As for raw dried beans, oats, rice, barley, sweet potatoes, beets and turnips, these have enzyme inhibitors that may disrupt a cockatiel's digestive system temporarily. Cook these before serving in order to deactivate harmful compounds.

## 4.    Preparing your house for the new arrival
Before you bring your beloved bird to your house, first you have to find a proper place for it. This place has to be quiet and without any air currents. The cage has to be equipped with all the necessary things: food, water and toys.

The first day it's better to offer a little bit of privacy to the bird, even if we like to watch it, and it is recommended to cover the cage, especially during the day. If you already own birds, the newly arrived bird has to be isolated in a separate cage (cages which are usually used for the transportation of the bird). You have to leave the bird to get used with the new conditions and to you.

A parrot is considered to be accommodated when it doesn't get scared at the appearance of the owner, when s/he is feeding properly and when its feathers look normal.

After the accommodation process, when you want to move your bird in another cage with the other birds, instead of stressing the bird by catching it with your hands, bring closer the entrances of the two cages and leave them in this position for a while to give your bird the chance to get into the other cage whenever s/he wants and when it is totally relaxed.

## 5.　　The transportation of the parrots

Transportation of the birds can be dangerous when it's done improperly and can cause serious problems to your bird.

When you transport your bird from your vet or from a pet shop to your home it is recommended to keep it in a special cage without water and food bowls in it, or in special carton boxes with tiny holes in them for the bird to be able to breath and to avoid accidents. If you choose the cage, you better cover it with a piece of thin, dark colored material and make sure that it has a hole on the top for the holder of the cage. You can also transport your bird in a bigger shoebox with a lid. The box must present on the sides little holes, which are necessary for air circulation inside the box.

## 6.　　How to train your parrot

### *Talking and training*

The best time to start training a cockatiel is at the age of 7-10 months old. The most important thing that you have to do is getting your bird used with other people. You have to make sure that almost every day your parrot will have the chance to be in contact with new people, to experience new surroundings. All those experiences and interactions with other people must be a positive experience for him/her. Don't forget that a hand-fed cockatiel is more likely to talk than one reared by the parents.

If you really want to teach your parrot to talk, you'll have to be more patient, you'll have to speak very often with him/her, and your voice has to be very calm. The training lessons have to represent positive experiences for your parrot and they have to last for about 5-10 minutes, once or twice a day. It could be one hour after the bird wakes up and about one hour before the bird goes to sleep, because during daytime the bird is most active and when they are active they're less inclined to be open to training.

You have to combine training time with playtime, because you actually want to make the bird enjoy the training. You'll have to encourage your parrot with the right words like "well done" and you'll have to offer rewards every time s/he says the words right. Be aware, never yell or hurt your parrot when s/he is doing something wrong or you feel that s/he is stressing you out. The bird will lose its confidence in you and it will be very hard for you to regain it. For the first days, don't try to handle the bird, because the most important thing is to get used to each other.

Place the cage in the same room where you usually spend the most time. Talk to your bird as much as possible and when you change the water and food, try to do it by not stressing the bird out too much. Offer your bird small treats when it seems fine with you being there. After a few days you can leave the cage door open and hold out a treat, encouraging your bird to come sit in the cage door. Place some food in your hand and encourage the bird to eat from your palm. Your bird will realize that you are its best friend and s/he will come out of the cage and will learn to step up on your finger. Soon you will observe that your parrot will sit very comfortably on your shoulder, which means that s/he has accepted you.

Parrots, in general, love sitting on people's shoulders and love to chew things, which decreases their aggression and depression problems. They like to chew on your hair, they don't bite it off, they're just chewing on it because they enjoy it. One of the most important words for your parrot to learn is "step up". Even if s/he steps up on your finger without any previous command, it is recommended to say the words "step up" every time the bird is performing your command and you'll have to say "well done", "good girl" or "good boy" after that.

Some parrots do learn to talk very well, but first they learn to talk on their own by listening to human conversations and imitating sounds. So, the first thing you can do to encourage your parrot to talk is to repeat the words all the time.

To encourage your parrot to say specific phrases that you really want your parrot to repeat, try to say them on a regular basis. Talk to your parrot when s/he is concentrated on you, that is usually when his/her eyes are attentive. The first word that most parrots will learn is "hello", because that is the first thing they hear whenever someone walks into a room.

It's very important to reward and to answer to your parrot every time it's saying words or making sounds, even if they are correct or not. Don't scream at your bird when s/he is very loud. Watch out for what you say in front of your bird; parrots learn the words that you don't really want them to learn, too.

You can use clickers with success to achieve the best training results. Parrots usually learn faster when you're using a clicker. When you start training your bird, first give it a treat and at the same time say "well done" or click the clicker. Your parrot will associate these sounds with the treat. Once the bird makes the association between praise (click) and treat, you can delay the reward. If your parrot already knows the "step up" command, it's easy to teach him/her to say "hello". You'll have to raise your hand in front of the bird, just like you want the bird to step up on it. When s/he steps up say "well done" and give your bird the treat. Repeat this command a few times until the bird understands it. Once the bird has raised his/her leg on its own to get the treat, wait and give the treat only when the bird is raising its leg a little bit higher. You can also use very subtle signs with your hands if you want your parrot to answer back to you. You have to choose a sign and use it in the same way you use a command, followed by a treat or praise. Your bird will learn very fast every little movement of your fingers.

Teach your parrot to play basketball, using a miniature basketball hoop by picking up an "easy to hold" ball and passing it through the tiny basket. Show your bird the basketball and say "toss!" and then put the basketball through the hoop. Next, hand the ball to your bird and say "toss!" If your bird puts the ball through the hoop, say "Well done!" in a happy, excited tone.

### Rope climbing exercise

For this exercise you will need a cotton rope (about 2.5-3 meters long), make knots on it about every 15 cm. Attach the rope from the ceiling using a metal hook. Place the parrot on the floor at the end of the rope and say, "Climb the rope!". If your parrot doesn't want to climb upward on the rope, you will have to hold a treat at 20 cm above the bird, and gradually move the treat towards the top end of the rope. As soon as your bird gets to the top knot, say, "Well done!" and at the same time give it the treat. You can repeat this exercise 5-6 times in one session. If your parrot already knows how to perform the exercise, you can replace the treats with lots of encouraging words.

### How to train parrots to stop biting

When parrots feel threatened they will react in different ways, like screaming, flapping their wings, running away, hissing, biting, etc. There are several factors that can make parrots feel threatened like perturbing them when attention is not wanted, invading their territory, sudden movements, unexpected noises, jealousy, etc.

Parrots can also bite when protecting their mate. In captivity, your parrot will bond with you, so if your bird has chosen you for a mate, it may feel that unfamiliar persons or new pets appear as a threat to your safety. In these situations it is best to gradually introduce your bird to the new person or pet, allowing your bird enough time to accept the change.

Parrots who are going through hormonal changes during the breeding season or molting may become annoyed and moody, which may lead to biting. You should watch its body language during these periods and leave your bird alone when attention is not wanted. It's our natural behavior when a bird bites to put the bird down and then we start to yell at that bird. In this situation we reinforce the bird to bite us, because that brings the bird more and more attention.

When your young parrot tries to nibble on your ears, fingers or other body parts you should offer them an acceptable alternative to chew on: apple slice, carrot, block of wood, etc. If the method above doesn't work, gently blow in their face and in a firm voice tell them "no". All we want to do is to reinforce and reward good behavior, like doing interactive things, standing on your hand, playing quietly, that are positive and socially acceptable.

For example, choose a toy, a key or an object that could interest your parrot, when s/he is touching that object reward or praise your bird. After s/he seems to look that s/he understands that command, make it pick up that object. You have to repeat this game until your parrot will pick it up and bring you that object.

Training lessons have to be short, about 5-10 minutes, and to represent a positive experience for you and for your bird.

The rewards (treats) have to be small quantities, but also something that your bird will enjoy eating, like sunflower seeds, for example. If you offer big rewards to your bird, then s/he will spend too much time eating them and your training lesson will be interrupted for too long. If your bird bites you, try hard not to even yell out in pain, just take the bird, put it down and walk away. Your parrot will learn that when s/he bites you, s/he will lose your attention.

Make sure your bird has things available to play with so that s/he will not bite you. Your parrot can't eat and bite or shred toys and bite at the same time, so if you can anticipate the behavior from happening, regardless of what the behavior is (biting, screaming) and provide some sort of distraction for your bird, they will not bite.

### Learn to observe your parrot's body language
Parrots usually show us how they're feeling and what they're going to do by using their bodies in different ways, because they tend to communicate with us this way.

When they have their tail flared it means that they are excited or will bite you. If your parrot has all its feathers sticking out, with its wings held out from the body, then s/he could be ready to fight. A crest lying flat on the head indicates a sign of anger, for example, when you get too close to your parrot while eating. It will open its beak and will spread its legs apart for a firmer grip on the perch. You can interact with your parrot to prevent the bite when you observe these kinds of signs.

When your parrot is happy to see a friend of yours or another bird, then s/he might puff out all its feathers, wag its tail, move its beak up and down, or stretch one wing and one leg out from the side of the body. Your cockatiel's crest can be completely raised when it is excited or alarmed. This usually happens when a cockatiel hears unusual sounds.

When your cockatiel gets very small, it could mean that it is scared.

## 7.    Hot and Cold

***How to care for your bird during the cold season***
Exotic birds can't resist sudden weather changes (from sudden cold to sudden hot weather), so you'll have to maintain a constant temperature for them during winter. Parrots like humidity, so if the air condition of your house is very dry because of the heating system, it is recommended to spray your bird daily with a handheld spray bottle.

***How to care for your bird during the hot season***
Many people think that parrots feel "at home" in high temperatures, but bird owners have to be prepared for hot weather. The bird's body temperature is between 104-105.8 degrees Fahrenheit (40-41 degrees Celsius), therefore your bird will withstand temperatures that up to this level. Birds don't have sweat glands like we do, so they can't adjust their body temperature. When we perspire, the evaporation of the moisture on our skin cools us. There are several ways in which your bird can drop his own body temperature:

- Heat loss during panting: birds increase their breathing rate by breathing faster with the beak open. They have dry mouths and while we see them panting when they're overheated, they're reacting to the heat and this does not mean that they can combat it without our help. Their life could be in danger because they can become dehydrated by evaporation of water through the respiratory system (mouth, nostrils and lungs).

- Evaporation of water through the skin and feet

- Vibrating the neck structures.

Birds that are brought outside should be watched closely. If you observe that your parrot is holding its wings away from its body and is panting, then you have to bring it to cooler temperatures and give it a shower with water at room temperature. Using cold water on an overheated bird can cause organ damage, shock and even death.

Don't place the cage in direct sunlight, because your bird will need a shady place and humidity. You can attach a spray or sprinkler system to the top of the cage or of your aviary and you can also set a timer and cool down the cages to offer your bird a refreshing shower.

## 8.  Aviaries

Outdoor aviaries are more spacious than traditional cages and what's more important is that they allow parrots more space and offer a natural environment and fresh air.

An outdoor housing place is made up of two compartments: a net aviary (flight unit) and a shelter. The net aviary has to be made of galvanized steel mesh and it should be 19-gauge (19G) and a maximum dimension of 2.5 cm x 1.25 cm (1 x ½ in). Netting of this size should also help to keep rodents and snakes out of the aviary; these creatures may well eat the eggs and the birds as well.

To protect the aviary from predators such as rats, weasels, and cats you need to bury the galvanized wire mesh deeply (at least a foot) in the ground or you will need to lay down a solid base, constructed using blocks or bricks sunk into the ground.

Ideally, the floor should be of concrete, which is much easier to clean than grass. The aviary should have provisions for food, drinking water, bathing water, grit, perching, nesting and a place to hang a cuttlefish bone. During the day they will perch on twigs or wooden dowels and you can offer your bird pinecones, balls, chains, etc. to play with.

The dimensions of the flight have 4-5 meters in length (157,4 - 196,8 inches); up to 2 meters in height (78,74 inches); and between 1.2 and 1.8 meters wide (70,86 inches).

The perches should never be so thick that your birds cannot grip them adequately, nor so thin that the birds' front toes curl right round to the back. Perches can be constructed in the shape of a T, and fixed in the floor, or suspended by means of wire loops attached firmly to the aviary framework. Perches should not overhang feeding utensils, because these are likely to be soiled by droppings from above. None of the wood used for perches should have been recently sprayed with chemicals. Branches are sometimes soiled by other wild birds, so it's very important to wash them before use. In southern states of the USA, outdoor caging must be protected from opossums to prevent exposure to the parasite called Sarcocystis Falcatula, which can result in a fatal lung infection.

If you place potted plants in your aviary, the birds will spend a lot of time perching, picking and climbing, so you should provide non-poisonous plants. Here are a few plants and shrubs that will delight your birds, but remember any plant can cause harm if your bird consumes a large enough amount of it:

- Blackberry (Rubus fruticosus)
- Birch (Betula spp.)
- Marigold (Calendula officinalis)
- Lemon balm (Melissa officinalis)
- Elderberry (Sambucus nigra): in Autumn the berries will grow almost anywhere
- Snowberry (Symphoricarpos albus): the birds will find this plant fascinating
- Dog Rose (Rosa canina): it has scarlet hips and beautiful flowers
- Hawthorn (Crataegus monogyna): it is ideal for nesting
- Delphinium: the birds will enjoy the seeds of this plant
- Valerian (Centranthus ruber): can be planted anywhere, the roots have restraint effect on rats
- Sunflower (Helianthus multiflorus): can be planted anywhere
- Tree Mallow (Lavatera olbia): it has red flowers which grow up in July and August
- Holly ( Ilex aquifolium): birds will love this plant
- Oregon Grape (Mahonia aquifolium): that shrub will survive most ravages or soils
- Jasmine (Jasminum officinale): there are Summer and Winter varieties which will produce yellow or white flowers.

### Plants that could cause intoxication to your parrots:
- Rhododendron
- Flamingo Flower
- Snowdrop (Galanthus nivalis)
- Geranium or Stork's bills (Pelargonium)
- Bearberry (Rhamnus purshiana)
- Ivy (Hedera helix)
- Lesser celandine (Ranunculus ficaria)
- Deadly nightshade (Atropa belladonna)
- Tobacco (Nicotiana tabacum)

- Mistletoe (Viscum album)
- Philodendron (Monstera deliciosa)
- Wood spurge (Euphorbia amygdaloides)
- Autumn crocus (Colchicum autumnale)
- Avocado (Persea americana)
- Peach (Prunus persica)
- Tomato (Lycopersicon esculentum).

*Roofing*

The roof of the flight nearest to the shelter should be covered with translucent plastic sheeting. This will help the birds to sit outside when the weather is bad or very hot. The shelter can be roofed with marine plywood, with all the cracks being filled with a waterproof material and tarred over, before heavy-duty roofing felt is applied. This should overlap for several inches down the sides of the shelter. To ensure that the interior remains dry, guttering should be attached along the back of the sloping roof to carry the rainwater away from the aviary.

As well as toys, you'll have to provide some items that help to maintain the physical health of your bird:

- Swings and chains, which increase the capacity of movement
- Therapeutic perches that keep the bird's feet healthy
- Perches or any wooden objects which are good for chewing (if you neglect your bird by not offering him/her different objects to chew, it could lead to beak deformation);
- A bowl with fresh water for bathing
- Various nutritional supplements like cuttlefish bone, seashells, etc.

One of the best games that your parrot could play is when s/he has to get out a peanut hidden inside a tiny hole of a log. Your parrot has to chew the log to get inside and to get the peanut. This game makes your bird concentrate and work hard to eat.

You can also make your parrot happy by replacing the old toys and perches with new ones. In fact, toys and interactive games that make your bird work hard mentally and physically will keep your bird healthy and svelte. It is a natural instinct for cockatiels to destroy wood. Chewing is a natural way for your parrot to keep its beak in good condition. So you should provide them with wood, rawhide, paper and cardboard.

They also like noisy and interactive toys like wiffle balls, music boxes, baby rattles, shape interactive toys, etc. You can also use your imagination and create toys out of normal household items: large and clean stainless steel bolts and washers; large buttons; plastic straws; unscented cardboard rolls; popsicle and other wooden sticks; wrap a nut or treat into a piece of paper; plastic bottle caps with any inserts removed, etc.

You should change and rotate the toys every week to help keep your parrot interested and active. When introducing a new toy, do it slowly, because if you do it too quickly, your parrot will tend to shy away and very possibly never play with it. Their natural curiosity and wanting to see everything will encourage them to come and check out the new toy with you, so make sure they see you playing with it before attaching it into the cage

# Chapter 3. Grooming and General Upkeep

Cockatiels are some of the most charming and lovable birds you can have as a pet. Aside from being very sociable, these feathery companions are adorable and relatively clean. With proper care, your cockatiel will have a long and happy life, adding brightness to any bird-loving home.

These birds make excellent companions, but they need to be kept healthy and treated with respect. In this chapter you will learn how to care for your pet's health and keep it in top physical condition.

## 1.    Grooming

Cockatiels require plenty of grooming. The feathers of these cute birds need care in order to keep them clean. Most of the grooming is fortunately accomplished by the bird itself. You should keep your cockatiel and its living quarters extra clean and bacteria-free by lending a helping hand, of course.

Other grooming necessities like trimming your cockatiel's feathers are as vital as the bird's hygiene routine in some cases. Failing to trim the pet's feathers will make it less prone to bond and depend on you. There is, of course, the risk of your cockatiel escaping by flying away.

Read on to discover the grooming tasks you need to accomplish for a beautiful bird that enjoys your company.

### *Bathing Options*

Giving your cockatiel the chance to bathe is crucial. When your bird gets to bathe often, you help it avoid having dry skin. The water helps in softening the keratin coating that naturally occurs on fresh feathers. Making sure your pet gets regular bathing furthermore keeps the feathers looking attractive and clean.

Cockatiels are known to produce plenty of powder down, a naturally occurring powder that appears on the bird's feathers. These creatures produce more dust than any other type of bird. Bathing will significantly cut down the presence of feather dust. It's mandatory you control the amount of dust on your cockatiel since breathing in excess dust can make your pet ill.

- Pet birds must be allowed to have as many baths as they wish. Certain birds enjoy water and having a daily bath. Some cockatiels might simply tolerate a few spray baths on a weekly basis. Each bird will have its own personal bathing preferences.
- It's advisable for baths to occur in the morning, giving your cockatiel lots of time to dry off its body before bedtime. A damp bird can't possibly have a comfortable night's rest.
- Keep windows near your cockatiel's bathing area closed. These pets should always be kept from drafty areas, more so while they're taking a bath.
- Your cockatiel's feathers should be allowed to dry naturally after each bath. Never use a blow dryer. Not only will its loud sound frighten most birds, a rapid change of temperature is never a good idea for cockatiels. In case your pet is soaking wet, dry it off gently with a soft terry cloth towel.

### Ways to Bathe Cockatiels

These birds enjoy being sprayed with a light water mist. Spraying sessions let oils and other greasy substances run off the creature's feathers, leaving the birds clean.

One other way you can bathe your cockatiel is by using a wide, durable and shallow dish. You may use any appropriate container, one that can hold an inch of water. Fill up the container with tepid water and allow your cockatiel to roll around the water where it will most likely get the undersides of its wings wet.

You may find birdbath dishes at pet shops. Keep an eye out for birdbath dishes that come equipped with a mirror located at the bottom of the dish. The mirror is supposed to encourage your cockatiel to explore the water.

If you want to keep costs down, a simple and flat dish or pan you already own will work. The wider the dish, the more room your pet will have to enjoy baths. Place the dish or pan on a counter where you won't mind being drenched, such as a kitchen counter.

There is also the easy and fun option of giving your cockatiel a misting bath each day from outside the cage. Pet birds that don't like using bath dishes can get clean this way with ease. Use a brand new water mist bottle. Pet shops carry them or you can find a suitable bottle at a shop that sells garden supplies. When spraying your cockatiel, spray the water facing up into the air. This way the mist falls down on the cockatiel like rain, helping you to avoid spraying water roughly and directly into the bird's face.

Some cockatiels may initially be scared of the spray bottle because of the sound the spraying creates. You can help a jittery bird adjust slowly to the bottle. Days before you give the cockatiel its very first spray bath, spray water using the bottle around the cage each day. The goal is to get your pet used to the sound coming from the spray bottle. To take it a step further, a few days before the first spray bath you can spray your hair or hands in front of the cockatiel. This will make the bottle and the accompanying mist appear far less threatening in your pet's eyes.

Eventually your cockatiel will become so used to mist baths, it will begin to enjoy the sessions and want to get wet. You may find your bird raising its wings. This means the cockatiel wants to get the undersides of its wings wet. When this happens, mist your bird's wings on their front and back regions. After a misting bath, always empty the water out of the spray bottle and allow the bottle to fully dry. This way, bacteria won't be calling the spray bottle home.

It's not rare for cockatiels to love bathing under running water. There are some cockatiels that enjoy their baths right next to their owners in the shower. You can find special perches available for sale; perches that mount inside the wall of a bath so pet birds can mount them.

If you happen to be one of the lucky owners of a cockatiel who enjoys bathing with humans, ensure your pet never comes into contact with hot water or soap. Furthermore, the force of water coming directly from a showerhead can be too strong for a small creature like your cockatiel. The best water flow inside the shower for these pets is water that splashes from the wall onto the cockatiel.

### Nervous Bathers
There are some birds that are very jittery and nervous… anything new scares them. Even a simple task like bathing becomes a challenge when you're dealing with a stressed bird. If you have to work with such a cockatiel, don't push the bird too soon. You should approach your pet gently and encourage it to bathe until it realizes the activity can be fun and will leave them feeling good.

Whenever you notice your cockatiel try to take a bath in its water dish, place a plate of water inside your pet's cage. You may try to gently coax the bird out of its cage and offer it a spray mist bath. The sound of rain can make cockatiels crave bathing sessions. The same thing can happen thanks to the sound of running water coming from a faucet.

Each day, offer a nervous cockatiel a shallow plate filled with water. See if this helps encourage your bird to take a bath. If you want to use the spray mist method when bathing a scared bird, allow your pet to perch on your hand then hold the cockatiel over the bathroom sink. Let your pet see its image in the mirror. The bird will assume its image is another real cockatiel. Next, give the bird a few gentle mists of water.

Verbally praise your feathery pal for being good and not attempting to fly away from you. Have treats ready so you can reward your pet right after its first few bathing sessions. This will help instill in your pet's mind that bathing is a positive experience to enjoy.

Don't rush your bird into acquiring good bathing habits. Depending on the cockatiel's natural disposition, it will take as little as a few hours to even months before it accepts bathing willingly. By introducing various kinds of bathing methods to your cockatiel, you are gradually and gently teaching your pet how grooming can be fun and safe.

## 2.    Trimming the Feathers

To keep your cockatiel from escaping by flying away, it's vital for its wing feathers to be trimmed. Don't worry, if you don't feel comfortable enough doing this on your own, you can have a professional at a pet shop or your vet complete this task.

Like all birds, cockatiels will make an attempt to flee by flying when it's frightened. By making sure your pet's wings are trimmed, you will keep it from attempting to take flight. The good news is you can provide your bird with different levels of flight capability. The level of flight a bird has is determined by the amount of feathers clipped from the wings.

If you have a young cockatiel chick that hasn't learned how to fly, it's best to clip its wings gradually over time. Don't clip the wings of very young birds in one session. Birds that are allowed to naturally learn to fly, land and employ their own bodies to move around turn out to be more confident pets. By removing a bird's ability to take flight when it's too young, they can grow up nervous and even neurotic.

How do you clip the wings of a cockatiel that is just beginning to learn the art of flying? Clip just the two flight feathers located outside each of your pet's wing. The bird will be slowed down from this but the minimal clipping will allow it to continue to fly. A week later, follow up the task by clipping the next two feathers. Wait another week then clip another two feathers.

By following this schedule, your cockatiel will have lost its flying capabilities only when it's a grounded bird, one that has slowly but surely learned to control its movements by walking around. This should leave you with a confident bird that knows how to hop around and land, despite not having full flight capabilities.

Note: A good breeder will typically employ this clipping method before sending any of their cockatiels to its new home.

Cockatiels that have been clipped at a very young age will frequently end up with crash landings. These can break tail feathers or cause further injuries. That's why it's never advisable to clip too much at a time when your bird has yet to learn better motor skills. When you're doing the trimming task yourself, make an effort to clip the cockatiel's wing feathers in a symmetrical fashion. Do this by trimming both wings at an equal rate. This will keep your bird looking good and give it great balance. A bad clipping job will make moving a lot more difficult for the cockatiel.

How frequently should you clip your cockatiel's feathers? When choosing how many feathers to clip off and how often, you have to factor in your pet's environment. Does your bird stay in an aviary that comes furnished with its own safety area? If yes, allowing your pet to fly is fine and the flight capabilities will help the cockatiel get plenty of necessary exercise.
If you are planning on having your cockatiel join exhibitions, keep in mind that the judges will be taking the bird's total look into consideration. Most pet owners who like to show their cockatiels at exhibitions leave the wings unclipped.

Does your bird share a home with dogs or cats? The added danger the presence of other pets provides will mean you have to allow your cockatiel a chance to escape. Only clip enough feathers that leave some degree of flying capability.

If you're one of those owners who allows pet birds to fly inside the house, then obviously leave more wings unclipped. In this situation, the goal is to allow your bird to fly just slowly enough so it doesn't hurt itself from flying too rapidly indoors. If your bird has opportunities to go outside, or could possibly get through an opening left ajar, it's a wise move to provide a more severe clip. The last thing you need is a missing cockatiel that flew away.

Clipping may also help tame and calm down a territorial or bossy alpha male cockatiel. Giving him a pretty severe wing clipping can humble him down several notches. When you're starting to bond with a new adult cockatiel, it's also a smart move to give it a severe clipping. A severely clipped wing will make it easier to bond with a fully grown cockatiel since the lack of flight capabilities will make the bird more dependent on you, especially when your pet needs help moving around. In cases where you need to chase the bird, it won't have the chance to go far off and hurt itself.

Which feathers should you clip? Never clip beyond the 10 primary feathers found on your cockatiel's wings. If you would prefer to leave your pet with some flight abilities, clip fewer feathers. It is possible to clip the "secondary" feathers located farther down, thereby shortening them instead, though I don't recommend it.

It's important for cockatiels to receive wing exercises, especially if you decide to clip its feathers. Dedicate some time each day holding your pet's feet to get it to flap its wings. This way you're providing the cockatiel the opportunity to develop strong muscles in its chest since it's using whatever wing feathers are available.

Keep in mind it's never possible to fully ground cockatiels. These birds can get around well enough even with clipped wings. Even in birds whose ten primary flight feathers have been clipped from each of its wings, it's not a wise move to bring them outside while perched on your shoulder. Anything can trigger fear in birds. It can be the sound of a fast vehicle driving by your street or the noises of a wild animal outdoors. Once the cockatiel gets scared, it can suddenly take flight and risk injuring itself. If you insist on bringing your pet bird outside to get some sun or for whatever reason, bring your cockatiel out in a pet-carrying cage.

When clipping your cockatiel's wing feathers, do so one at a time. Always decide how many feathers to clip beforehand. You should also determine the level of flight capabilities that matches your bird's environment. Prior to trimming each wing feather, look at it closely. You will need to figure out whether it's a blood feather or not. Never clip blood feathers since clipping these will cause bleeding to occur. A blood feather has a feathered out tip but its base contains blood vessels and nerves. These blood feathers siphon blood and clipping at this level will cause injury and pain to your cockatiel.

If you do happen to accidentally clip a blood feather and bleeding ensues, sometimes the only method to stop the blood flow is pulling out the shaft. You can ask a vet to do this task. In pulling out the shaft of the injured blood feather, you need to place a firm grasp on the shaft and pull it quickly while supporting the bird's wing bones. Seek professional assistance whenever possible.

As you're clipping feathers, never leave long stray feathers. The feathers of cockatiels are naturally meant to grow together. Each feather supports another as it grows in. Leaving a long feather right at the tip of a wing leaves your bird with the chance of getting its feathers caught or entangled. By not clipping long stray feathers in the bird's wings, there is a higher chance of accidents or injuries occurring.

## 3.   Molting

The molting process can take place once or twice per year, which usually doesn't have any effect on the birds flying capacity.

The natural molting happens when the warm season ends and the colder season appears. In this period of the year birds will change all their feathers. The molting will take place gradually, in some birds it will take from 2 to 3 months (March - June) and it could happen after the birds have hatched their eggs and after rearing their youngsters. This process is influenced by the hormones of thyroid gland and the genital organs. In this period they'll need a proper diet like camomile tea (Matricaria Chamomilla), St John's wort tea

(Hypericum Perforatum), amino acid like methionine, hemp seeds and vitamins like A, D, E.

They also become very stressed when molting takes place, and it makes them vulnerable to new diseases. In this period they're cleaning themselves persistently and have a quieter disposition. When normal molting is taking place, there should never be bald patches present on the bird's body. The new feathers that are replacing the old feathers are called blood feathers. If the blood feather is cut or injured it can bleed in excess. If your bird has broken blood feathers, you'll have to ask for your avian vet for help. All s/he has to do is to pull the broken feather out and apply some pressure with a gauze square to stop the bleeding. When your parrot is molting it could have many pinfeathers present, especially on the back of its head because a parrot can't preen the normally present feather sheaths from the back of the head. You can help your parrot by removing gently the feather sheaths with your index finger and thumb. You have to be very careful when you are doing this, because it could be very painful for your bird.

## 4.    Microchipping your cockatiel

A microchip is a very small electronic device encased in a glass chamber, about the size of a grain of rice, which is inserted into a bird. When a scanner is passed over the area of the body containing the chip, it is activated and it transmits an identification number and the name of the chip manufacturer to the scanner's display screen. The person scanning, using the manufacturer database, will locate the contact information of the owner.

Make sure the scanned microchip number matches the number on the computerized paper strip that goes in the brochure which the client takes home. You can also ask your avian vet to check periodically the proper functionality of the microchip. The microchip is implanted into the pectoral muscle of the bird or under the wings (on the left side). The procedure is much like an injection and it last about 10 seconds; the chip is implanted through a hypodermic needle. It can be done without the use of anesthetics, but many vets prefer to anesthetize to ensure proper placement. If you are changing your address and phone number, don't forget to remind your vet or specialist from the animal shelter to register your new address.

Microchips are not GPS devices, they're for the purpose of identifying found birds. Birds that are found and taken to the animal shelters are scanned for microchips before they're adopted. It is recommended that you use a widely known brand, increasing the probability that a scanner for that brand is available.

## 5.    First aid kit for your cockatiel

It's very important to have a first aid kit in your house, because sadly accidents can happen. First you'll have to call your avian vet, but you have to be ready to use your first aid kit in case your bird requires immediate medical care in cases like burns or injury of one of the wings.

The first aid kit has to contain the following items:
- Electric birds pillow, to warm up the bird to treat shocks; don't leave it unattended on the pillow, because there is a danger of overheating.
- Pedialyte (electrolyte solution for children), these kind of solutions have to be given at room temperature.
- Eye drops (medication) and eye wash (to clean the eyes).
- Eyedropper.
- Cotton swabs and balls to clean open wounds.
- Scissors.
- Gauze rolls to bandage scratches, burns or open wounds.
- Tweezers to remove broken blood feathers.
- Antiseptic wipes.
- Betadine or iodine solution.

- Medical tape.
- Masking tape.
- 3% hydrogen peroxide solution to clean wounds. When you clean the wound for the first time, you'll have to use the undiluted form of the solution. After that you'll have to dilute the hydrogen peroxide solution with water 1:10.
- Medical first aid pen flashlight, to see inside of the bird's mouth.
- Antibiotic ointment to prevent infection of cuts and scratches.
- Syringe (without needle on top), feeding tubes, pipettes. You have to be well prepared before you use feeding tubes.
- Towels.
- Hand-feeding formula.
- Latex gloves.
- Animal poison control center phone number.
- Magnifying glass.
- Heating lamp.
- Bird's medical records.
- Parrot's first aid book.

# Chapter 4. Common Health Problems

Although we shall of course always do our best to maintain the stellar health of our beloved pet, there can be instances where our cockatiels become ill. It is important for us as carers to know how to spot diseases and illnesses in order to nip them in the bud or act accordingly.

### *The first sign of disease*
There are several physical and behavioral signs that a bird is not feeling well:

- Depressed attitude and unusual irritability.
- They sleep more than 10-12 hours per day, with their head hidden under the wing.
- They keep their eyes almost shut all the time and the wings hang from the body.
- They don't have the same stability on their legs and they spend more time than usual on the bottom of the cage.
- Their appetite is reduced and they are losing weight.
- They don't clean their plumage or feet.
- Excessive cough and sneeze and nose secretions.
- The feathers around the beak and the vent are dirty.
- Eye discharge or swollen eyes.
- Their feces are a different color to normal and they have diarrhea.
- Excessive molting.
- Discoloration of feathers.
- Breathing difficulties.

When you recognize these signs, you should contact your vet doctor for a precise diagnosis.

### *Some advice about how to keep your birds healthy*

- The most important condition to keep your birds healthy is a proper diet.
- Choosing the appropriate cage and the right environment are very important factors.
- The cage must be kept clean to avoid bacterial infestation.
- Daily flying exercises are needed in order to keep the muscles strong. This is as easy as letting the bird out of the cage once in a while and encouraging it to attempt to fly (even if his wings are clipped).
- Watch out for poisonous plants.
- Cigarette smoke, hair spray (hair lacquer), body spray, furniture spray and vapors of household cleaners like bleach should be avoided when the birds are around.
- Learn about the natural habits of your bird, for example, you can find out if your bird loves to have bath more often than showers, then you have to place a bowl filled with water in the cage, or for the other option you'll have to spray him/her with water very often.
- Take the bird to the vet regularly, because birds can hide the signs of diseases. In the wild sick birds hide any sign of their disease, they even try to eat with the rest of the flocks, because there is a risk of losing their life (the others will steal his food and bite him because they feel his weakness). The cage birds can act the same way, they look like they are healthy, they eat very well, until one day they could fall off the perch. Even when they have sharp pains, they don't tend to exteriorize their feelings. The bird plumage can hide the eventual weight losses caused by diseases.

- The main cause of diseases suffered by birds is accidents. The birds left unattended and can hit the windows or cut themselves on different kind of objects.
- Maintain a stable body temperature. The normal body temperature of these birds is 105.8 degrees Fahrenheit (41 degrees Celsius). If the body temperature is above or below this, the bird is sick.
- When the birds are sick they usually refuse to eat, this could be a big problem because they can't survive for long without food. It is therefore necessary to force your bird to eat, with viscous consistency mashed food, which is given little by little, with a syringe without needle on top. You can feed your parrot for 3-4 times per day with approximately 5-10 ml of liquid food.

In the following sections we will go into great detail about the specific health conditions that can be found in cockatiels as well as their symptoms and treatment.

## 1.    Parasites

### External parasites

External parasites or ectoparasites are mostly lice or mice. Lice infestations appear as small, brownish colored insects that can be seen moving through your bird's feathers. Sometimes you can't see lice with the naked eye, you just simply notice excessive itching in your bird. Bird lice lay their eggs at the base of the feather and the egg developing period could take up to 6 weeks.

### a) Cnemidocoptes

The most common mite seen on birds is Cnemidocoptes - the Scaly Face/Leg mite, which feeds on keratin, the protein that makes up the surface layer of the skin, beak and feet.

*Symptoms:*

- Left untreated, the Scaly Face mite can cause disruption of the growth areas of the beak, leading to distortion of the beak.
- Thickening of the scales on the legs can lead to pain.
- With a massive infestation, there can be total or partial loss of feathering.

*Treatment:*

- Combatting parasites can be done with Ivermectin or Moxidectin, which can be applied to the skin on the back of the neck or put in the bird's drinking water. This type of parasite doesn't have any effect on humans.

*Internal parasites*
### b) Gapeworm (Syngamus Trachea)

This is a disease caused by a worm called Syngamus trachea, which is located in the trachea of the affected bird. The gapeworm also affects turkeys, geese, caged birds and wild birds, especially wild pheasants. Infestation occurs when there are wild pheasants close to your birds or indirectly by intermediate hosts like earthworms and snails.

Gapeworms are located in the trachea, bronchi and the lungs. Gurgling noises that come from the throat of the bird are caused by the gapeworm infestation, and it can be confused with respiratory problems.

*Symptoms:*

- Difficulty breathing with open beak
- Cough
- Anemia
- Anorexia
- Weakness

- If there is a heavy infestation of gapeworms, the bird could die of suffocation.

*Treatment:*
- Thiabendazole powder in feed.
- Fenbendazole (Panacur) for 3 days. Flubendazole for youngsters in feed for 7 days.
- Febantel (Rintal) in feed for 7 days.
- Tetramisole-Nilverm administered in water for 3 days.
- Disinfection and dry maintenance of the aviary or cage is required.

### c) Trichomoniasis (Trichomonas gallinae)
This parasite is located in the sinuses, mouth, throat, crop, intestine and liver of the bird. In addition to domestic birds, there are also wild birds which are infested with this kind of internal parasite (sparrows, vultures, seagulls, wild doves, etc.).

*Symptoms:*
- White or yellow cheesy-looking nodules inside of the mouth and throat
- Reduced appetite
- Excessive mucus in the mouth, esophagus and crop
- Vomiting
- Dehydration
- Weight loss
- Diarrhea
- Respiratory disorders
- Even death.

*Treatment:*
You must gently remove the cheesy deposits from the bird's mouth and apply some tincture of glycerin-iodine solution (1%trypaflavine).

- Trichomonas gallinae is very contagious disease and can spread through the beak (when they feed each other), food and drinking water. If the disease is recognized in time (is located only in the crop and the mouth), then immediate treatment with Dimetridazole is required.
- Dimetridazole for 3-5 days.
- Metronidazole (Flagyl) twice daily for 5-6 days.
- Ronidazole for 7 days.

You must separate the infected birds from the others. The cage and the accessories must be disinfected with hot water.

### d) Histomoniasis
This is caused by parasites (Histomonas meleagridis) that affect the ceca and the liver of the bird. The youngsters are more exposed to this kind of infection.

*Symptoms:*
- Excrements yellow in color.
- Walking disorders caused by the inflammation of the joints.

*Treatment:*
- Administration of Dimetridazole; Ronidazole; polivitamines.
- It can be prevented by the disinfection of the cage or aviary through flaming and the control of humidity. Periodical disinfection of the feeding and water bowls is required and preventive administration of Dimetridazole in food is necessary.
- In this period it is good to administer some probiotic supplements (containing beneficial bacteria), which will help to rebuild the intestinal flora of the bird.
- Healthy greens and veggies will also help.

### e) Eimeria (Coccidiosis)

This is a disease which is produced by parasites developing in the bird's intestinal tract. There are 9 species of Coccidia which belong to the genus Eimeria and can infect different parts of the intestine: Eimeria tenella, Eimeria acervulina, Eimeria mivati, Eimeria mitis, Eimeria necatrix, Eimeria maxima, Eimeria brunetti, Eimeria praecox and Eimeria hagani. It could affect youngsters between 10 days and three months old.

*Symptoms:*
- Diarrhea with bloody mucous in it
- Pink intestinal tissue in droppings
- Lack of appetite
- Slow growth
- Anemia.

*Treatment:*
The treatment is more effective if it's done in the first days of disease. Most of the medications must be added in water.
- Treatments with sulfonamides will have to be associated with vitamin K3 to prevent hemorrhagic phenomenon caused by sulfaquinoxaline.
- Treatments with Amprolium (Thiamine) last for 5-7 days, and have a reduced toxicity.
- It's also good to administer some polivitamins, to your birds.
- Maintaining hygiene and proper food prevents diseases.

**f) Ascariasis**
This is a parasitic disease caused by parasites (Ascaridia), which affects 3-4 months old young birds, turkeys, geese, pigeons, parrots, etc. Ascaridia galli is a white-yellowish colored worm.
Youngsters can get infected orally through infested water or feed. Massive infestation with worms could lead to the blockage of the intestine causing death if it's not treated.

*Symptoms:*

- Weakness
- Anorexia
- Diarrhea
- Anaemia
- Hypovitaminosis
- Youngsters stop developing.

*Treatment:*

- Piperazine salts are effective in treatments against ascariasis.
- Cambendazole in feed for 5 days.
- Fenbendazole (Panacur) in feed for 4 days.
- Mebendazol in feed for 7 days.
- Flubendazole in feed for 7 days.
- Disinfection of the cage or aviary through flaming and periodical disinfection of birds is required.

## g) Toxoplasmosis

Toxoplasmosis is an infection caused by the parasite Toxoplasma gondii.

*Symptoms:*

- Fever
- Respiratory dysfunction
- Diarrhea
- Paresis
- Paralysis
- Convulsions.

*Treatment:*

- Administration of sulfonamides
- Antibiotics
- disinfection through flaming.

## 2.    Skin and Feather Problems

Massive molting represents the slow growth process of feathers. The affected birds have broken and disintegrated feathers.

There are multiple causes like food deficiency (the lack of amino acids, vitamins and minerals), improper maintenance (insufficient light and humidity), liver or kidney disease, tumor or hormonal disorders.

Soft molting is a permanent or partial feather loss of the bird. The most important causes are high levels of humidity with light and food deficiency.

French molting is characterized by the continuous growth and loss of feathers without the possibility to cover all parts of the bird's body. There are a few possible causes that produce the French molt, like viruses (Polyoma or Circoviruses, which have the potential to inflame feather follicles), environment changes, hereditary problems, parasites and nutrition problems. If you notice patches of bare skin on your bird's body or the molting process is not running normally, then you should visit your avian vet as soon as possible.

### a) Inflammation of the skin (Dermatitis)

Inflammation of the skin could appear among other diseases like renal diseases with increasing levels of uric acid in the blood, liver disease or infestation with external parasites.

*Symptoms:*
- Flaky or scaly skin
- Excessive itching
- Occasional blood when scratched
- Irritation around eyes and ears
- Oozing eyes.

*Treatment:*

You can use the following therapeutic measures:

- Applying astringent and disinfectant solution on the wet wounds. Do not use ointments, because the feathers will become greasy and the bird can peck the wounds.
- There are injections with antibiotics which stops the bacterial infestations. Injections with multivitamins and immune system boosters can help the bird to fight against diseases.
- In case that there are itchiness problems, it would be recommended to use some special anesthetic powder for external use on the affected areas on the skin. In this case the skin will be anaesthetized and the itchiness should disappear.
- When there is the possibility of massive bleeding (because the bird is scratching too much the affected areas) a collar should be applied around the bird's neck. In some cases the bird won't be happy about the collar, especially if the itchiness was caused by physical problems (stress), and maybe this solution (collar) will not resolve the problem.

## b) Xanthomas (Fatty tumors)

Xanthoma is a skin disease that affects overweight birds, especially parrots. Beneath the skin there are deposits of fatty tumors, which have a yellowish color and they can be found in chest area, the wing tips, and in ventral and femoral regions (between the legs and around the vent). These encapsulated benign tumors are composed of mature fat cells. The affected areas can be easily damaged or ulcerated, especially as it gets bigger. Birds will cause self-trauma by pecking them.

*Treatment:*

- Xanthoma is a very common disease in birds that are fed exclusively on seeds. You'll need to introduce in the bird's diet some millet, fruits, herbs, green leafy veggies.

- Once the bird get all the necessary food, the existent fatty deposits will stop developing.
- The eczema should be disinfected with an antiseptic solution.

### c) Skin tumors (Lipomas)

Skin tumors can appear on all species of birds. The most common tumors are lipomas, which are fatty tumors that can develop beneath the skin, and could appear on the stomach or chest area. It can also develop internally.

A common cause of lipomas is obesity and vitamin E deficiency.

### *Treatment:*
- The proper treatment is low-fat diet.
- If the lipoma is big and painful or infected your vet will surgically remove the tumor, because this is the best option for your bird's health.

## 3.    The appetite and the digestive system

### a) Diarrhea

When a bird has diarrhea, the droppings are very soft even fluid, with a smell different from normal. The frequency of elimination of droppings will be very high. These are the only symptoms.

Diarrhea leads to dehydration of the bird and to loss of minerals of the organism. There are multiple causes such as inadequate nutrition, bacterial infection of the intestines, intoxications, parasites, etc.

### *Treatment:*
- The required treatment is focused on an antidiarrheal diet and specific medication for each situation.
- You will need to feed your bird some poppy seeds because of their calming effect, boiled rice; some fried seeds and replace

water with mint tea. You can add to mashed boiled rice some coal powder.

- Antidiarrheal medication will be followed after your avian vet advice. You can also offer to your bird instead of water a special solution that contains minerals and it could be prepared at pharmacies:

| | |
|---|---|
| NaCl (sodium chloride) | 8.0 g |
| CaCl2 (calcium chloride) | 0.13 g |
| KCl (potassium chloride) | 0.2 g |
| MgCl (magnesium chloride) | 0.1 g |
| NaH2PO4 (monosodium phosphate) | 0.05 g |
| NaHCO3 (sodium bicarbonate) | 10 g |
| Glucose | 1.0 g |
| Distilled water | 1000.0 ml |

It's very important to separate your bird from the others, to assure an adequate temperature of the room 77 - 95 degrees Fahrenheit (25 - 35 degrees Celsius) and very strict hygiene.

## b) Enteritis (Inflammation of the intestines)

Enteritis is the inflammation of the intestines and it's one of the most frequent causes of mortality in cage and aviary birds.

The main causes of enteritis are malnourishment, intoxications, intestinal parasites, tapeworms, eelworms, coccidia that harms the intestinal mucus, viruses and bacterial infections. Salmonellosis and E. coli are pathogenic bacterias which are the main causes of the enteritis.

## Symptoms:

- The main symptom of the enteritis is diarrhea.
- The feathers around the cloaca are dirty.
- The bird is lethargic, sad and sleeps too much.

- Because it has lost too much liquid, the affected bird will drink a lot of water.

*Treatment:*
- The bird has to be placed in a warm place.
- It will need infusions and forced feeding.
- Injection with vitamins will strengthen the immune system of the bird.
- The avian vet will prescribe the proper antibiotic treatments for your bird.

### c) Gastrointestinal parasites - Tapeworms

Tapeworms live in the bird's body and eliminate their eggs through the bird's feces. The eggs are consumed by intermediate hosts (earthworms, snails and insects like grasshoppers, ants, beetles, flies, etc.). Inside the intermediate hosts a small embryo develops in the eggs but does not hatch immediately. When the bird is eating the infected insects or worms the larvae in the egg reaches the infective stage within two to three weeks and they will become tapeworms in the bird's body.

*Symptoms:*
- Similar to all gastrointestinal problems, which makes it so hard to diagnose until proper tests have been carried out.

*Treatment:*
- Wild parrots are infested with tapeworms when they eat insects and worms directly from the wild. Wild parrots that were recently imported (captured from the wild) could have a prophylactic treatment against the tapeworm with Praziquantel.
- Infestation with tapeworms is uncommon in domestically raised parrots.

## d) Obesity

Obesity could lead to health problems like heart and circulatory system disorders, joint problems, modification of the internal organs like liver fattening and constipation. The major problems are the impossibility of flying, loneliness, and overfeeding with flax and rape seeds. The main measures that must be taken are the introduction of lettuce in the bird's diet and to increase the frequency of free flight in the room. You can replace the drinking water with dandelion tea for 20 days. The obese bird will have to receive only half of the usual daily seeds portion. Green food and fruits can be offered daily.

## e) Excessive weight loss

The excessive weight loss of the bird could have multiple causes like nutritional and parasitic problems. The suffering bird has dry skin and a very prominent breastbone.

When you observe these symptoms, you'll have to disinfect the cage and the bird, and get droppings samples for further examinations. Your avian vet will provide a diagnosis and will establish the treatment.

## 4.    Liver diseases

### a) Inflammation of the liver (Hepatitis)

The main factors that trigger acute chronic hepatic inflammations are bacteria, viruses, funguses, parasites or intoxications. The liver is increasing in size, but it's an organ with incredible regeneration power if the disease is discovered in time. If the hepatic tissue is very affected, then it can't regenerate cirrhosis of the liver occurs. The possible cause could be perishable oily seeds. Hazelnut mold (Aspergillus flavus) that forms in wet weather on the nutshell is extremely toxic for the liver. You'll have to check the quality of the nuts before you offer it to your bird, by tasting them. Try to use brands that are sold with success in stores and supermarkets, this way you'll have the chance to buy fresh nuts.

*Symptoms:*
- The affected birds look tired, lethargic and with lack of appetite.
- The affected liver is not able to help much the body with detoxification.
- Most birds suffer from itching.
- Feather plucking.
- The urine color is white and the feces are greenish-yellow.

*Treatment:*
- Curing cirrhosis is impossible, but its evolution can be stopped when it is recognized in time.
- Treatments with liver protection medication could be done.

**b) Fatty liver**
This is a disease which appears especially in overweight birds. The accumulation of fat excess in the liver cells makes the liver work improperly.

*Symptoms:*
- Diarrhea
- Respiratory difficulties
- The nails and the beak are overgrown.
- When the liver increases too much in size, the tissue of the liver could break up and internal bleeding could appear, causing death.

*Treatment:*
- To avoid these kinds of situations, slow weight loss is needed by reducing the consumption of oily seeds, administration of vitamin E and liver protection medication and lots of exercise

86

is recommended (outdoor flying) to regenerate the liver function.

## 5.     Beak health problems
### a) Deformed beak
When the owners don't offer cuttlefish bone to their birds, their beak will overgrow, which will lead to the impossibility of the bird eating and drinking. If the beak is not cut back in the appropriate time, the bird could die, due to the impossibility of feeding itself.

*Symptoms:*
- The abnormal growth of the beak, in some cases, could be because of a serious health disorder.
- Discolored beak.
- Asymmetrical beak.
- No refusal to eat, but rather a struggle is visible when trying to eat.

*Treatment:*
- You'll have to replace the soft food with the right diet and offer some tree branches to your bird to chew.
- Some owners used to cut their parrot's beak even if it's unnecessary, this way they will accelerate the growing process of the beak.

### b) Soft beak
The beak of some birds becomes very flexible because of a vitamin and calcium deficiency. The main cause is vitamins A, C, biotin, pantothenic acid, folic acid and calcium or phosphorus deficiency.

*Symptoms:*
- Sometimes the beak may appear to have scales on it.
- Asymmetrical beak.
- Misaligned beak.

- Difficulty eating.

*Treatment:*
- You'll have to grease the bird's beak with vitamin A or cod-liver oil.
- Administer some calcium and crushed eggshells.

# 6.    Respiratory system problems

The loud whistling sounds and hard breathing of the bird indicates a problem with its respiratory system. The birds are very sensitive to air currents and they get cold very easy. To prevent these kinds of problems, you'll need to find a proper place for the cage.

When you hear this whistling noise, you must feed the bird grated carrots and fruits and green plants rich in vitamin C.

### a) Syngamus trachealis

This disease is caused when a gapeworm infects the tracheas of a bird. These are red worms and are mostly found in young birds.

*Symptoms:*
- The bird will gasp for air.
- Breathing with the mouth open.
- Outstretched neck.
- Wheezing sounds when breathing.

*Treatment:*
- This disease can be prevent with proper sanitation and regular cleaning of the cage.
- Administration of Flubendazole (Flubenvet) or benzimidazole.

### b) Acute respiratory insufficiency

Respiratory insufficiency is a symptom that usually appears from many and different kinds of health disorders. Respiratory difficulties can develop after the modification of the internal organs, which are pressing the airways. When the thyroid gland increases in size, it can restrain the airways. All the internal organs are situated in the same cavity of the body (thoracic cavity and stomach are not separated by a diaphragm as in mammals), and the modification of the internal organs may influence negatively the respiratory functions. The normal function of the air sacs and the lungs is affected by the increase of the liver, by obesity, sexual disorders and the accumulation of excrements as a result of digestive diseases.

*Symptoms:*
- When it's a slow evolution process of the disease, the affected bird is flying less.
- Lethargy because of the lack of oxygen.
- The affected bird is breathing rapidly with an open beak.

*Treatment:*
- If the bird is not taken to the vet for consultation and treatment, the bird could suffocate.
- One must determine the underlying illness causing acute respiratory insufficiency in order to treat it.

## c) Rhinitis

Rhinitis is an inflammation of the nostrils that can lead to serious respiratory problems if left untreated. The main cause of rhinitis is infection with viruses, bacteria or mycoplasmosis. Rhinitis is transmissible from parrot to human.

*Symptoms:*
- The feathers around the nostrils are dirty, because of the abundant nose secretions.
- The nasal discharge can form a crust and can block the nasal orifices.

- The bird rubs his head on perches and on different objects of the cage to liberate his/her affected nostrils.

## Treatment:
- The avian vet will administer an injection with antibiotic (Tetracycline).
- In case that the infection is resistant to Tetracycline, laboratory investigation is needed to find the proper antibiotic for the bird.
- Injections with Poly Vitamins are also indicated and vitamin C powder, (a pinch of vitamin C powder in 30 ml of water) added in drinking water to fight the infection.
- The nostrils and the feathers around it will have to be cleaned with cotton wool soaked in warm water, few times per day.
- The inflamed and red skin around the nostrils has to be greased with a special ointment, which contains fish grease, marigold (Calendula officinalis) and vitamin A.
- Because the body temperature of the bird drops, you'll have to warm it up by placing a heat lamp or bulb (60-100W) near the cage. The "warming up " procedure has to be done until the bird is recovering. You can also place a bowl filled with hot chamomile infusion in front of the cage. You'll have to cover the cage with a towel and try to direct the hot streams inside the cage. You can apply this method once or twice per day.
- Disinfection with hot water of the perches, feeding and drinking bowls is required. Rhinitis could affect birds that live in preheated rooms, especially during winter. Because of the dry air, the bird's airways become affected. To control the humidity of the room, you can place a wet towel on the radiator. There is also special humidifying equipment or you may also offer your bird the opportunity to have baths every day. You can also spray your bird daily with warm water.

# 7.    Reproduction problems

## a) Egg retention

A frequent problem in caged birds is the retention of the egg. If the hen can't lay the egg, it could press on the internal organs. The impossibility to eliminate droppings could lead to self-intoxication. It can happen because of the age of the bird, the size and shape of the egg, the sudden drops of temperature 53.6 degrees Fahrenheit (12 degrees Celsius) and the stress during the egg laying process.

*Symptoms:*

- Depression.
- Wide stance.
- Loss of appetite.
- Distended abdomen.
- Bobbing of the tail
- Lameness or paralysis of the legs in severe cases due to the egg pressing on nerves.

*Treatment:*

- At the first signs of the retention of the egg, wet heat will help in most cases. You'll have to place a bowl filled with hot water in front of the cage, which must be covered with a towel and the hot steams have to be directed towards the cage.
- A heating lamp or bulb (60W) will be necessary near the cage and directed towards the suffering bird.
- You can also help your bird by introducing 0.5-1 ml of warm oil in the cloacal orifice. This operation should continue each hour until the egg is delivered. In this case, for the bird's safety, veterinary intervention is required.
- The temperature in the room has to be maintained around 86 degrees Fahrenheit (30 degrees Celsius).

### b) Infertility of the cock

One of the main causes of infertility of the cock is the unsuitable partner and for this reason the birds need to be watched during the mating period.

*Symptoms:*
- Stress.
- Inadequate feeding.
- Too young or too old to mate.

*Treatment:*
- During the mating period, the cock's diet must have more vitamin E.

## 8.     Nervous system problems

### a) Twirling or Torticollis

There could be several causes including infections with viruses, bacteria, parasites, and mycoplasma, as well as intoxication, brain injuries and a lack of vitamin A and Calcium.

*Symptoms:*
- They constantly throw their head back.
- They walk around in circle.
- The ability to turn their head around in a circle.
- Constantly looking up

*Treatment:*
- If there are cerebral diseases, the bird needs to stay in a dark and quiet place on a piece of soft cloth to keep it comfortable during the treatment administered by the vet.
- Treatment will depend entirely on the cause.

# 9. Foot and limb problems

## a) Abscess of the feet

The main causes of this disease are the circulatory disorders of the feet caused by insufficient movement, inappropriate perches and lack of vitamin A.

*Symptoms:*

- First the abscess forms on the heel or under a toe (a pressure zone).
- The skin becomes very thin, the wound appears and soon it will be covered with crust.
- The affected foot is swollen and is very warm.
- The wound becomes an open injury filled with pus.

*Treatment:*

- The crust has to be removed surgically and the affected foot will be treated with medicated ointment.
- The affected bird will be supervised for 10 days. The bandage has to be changed at every 2-3 days.
- Injection with multivitamins stimulates the healing process.
- To spare the other foot, the perches must be wrapped with paper towels or with bandages and they have to be fixed at the end of perches with adhesive tape. All the perches available in the cage have to be wrapped, because the bird will hesitate to sit on them.
- If there are not pustules filled with pus on the bird's foot, it's enough to use ointment with vitamin A or with fish fat (grease) daily. During this treatment the presence of grit is not necessary in the cage, because it will stick on the bird's foot and it will stop the healing process.
- Offer your bird the opportunity of free flight every day for 1-2 hours. This way the circulatory system and the blood circulation in the feet will be stimulated. The lack of

movement and the overweight body of the bird has negative effects on the feet.

## b) Sprains and dislocations

Sprains and dislocations appear after the wrong manipulation of the bird or its leg is stuck between the bars.

*Symptoms:*
- The affected joints are inflamed, causing pain.
- The affected area is increasing in size.

*Treatment:*
- In the case of sprains, the treatment consists in the application of a bandage with wool balls soaked in alcohol and the settlement of the bird in quiet place is required.
- In the case of a dislocation, re-suspend the ends of the joints in the initial position and then maintain them in this position by applying around the hip joint an adhesive tape.
- You can feed your bird poppy and hemp seeds, and everyday observation of the bird is required.

## c) Fractures

Fractures appear as a result of accidents through manipulation or bumping of the bird.

*Symptoms:*
- The leg is dragged and the opposite extremity of the fracture moves.
- The affected area is turgid, much bigger, infiltrated with blood and lymph.
- If the fracture is open, then there is a rupture of the muscle and skin, with the visibility of bones.

*Treatment:*

- The treatment has to be done in maximum 48 hours after the accident.
- Calming the pain with infiltration of pain killers.
- Disinfection of the area with ethacridine lactate (Rivanol solution).
- Removal of impurities.
- Immobilization of the area .
- Attach a collar around the bird's head to prevent tearing the bandage.
- Administration of antibiotics and vitamins, daily.
- Supervision of the evolution of the fracture.

## d) Gout

When uric acid level becomes too high in the bird's blood stream, gout occurs. Birds usually don't produce too much urine. The uric acid is removed from the blood by the kidneys and eliminated through the urine. When the kidneys don't work properly, the level of uric acid becomes too high in the blood stream and it will become crystallized.

*Symptoms:*

- In articular gout, the uric acid crystallizes in the joints, ligaments and tendon sheaths, forming white nodules, which could be very painful. The feet are swollen and become red-violet color. When the uric acid crystallizes in tissues, it will form small, white nodules.
- In visceral gout, uric acid deposits are found in the liver, kidneys, spleen and air sacs.

*Treatment:*

- High dose of vitamin A, lots of fluids and stimulation of renal function by adding in drinking water sucrose (sugar) could positively influence the evolution of disease.
- Because of the swollen feet and painful nodules the bird may be unable to perch and so it will remain on the floor of the cage. The food and water bowls should be placed to be easily accessible locations, by helping the bird to be able to eat and drink without any problem.
- The perches have to be wrapped with paper towels and the cage has to contain little wrapped platforms to help the bird sit comfortably.
- Nodules could be eliminated surgically when they have a specific size. In this case anesthesia is not recommended, because it could harm the affected kidneys.

## 10.  Intoxication

Intoxication deserves its own section because we must realise that our own mistakes can seriously harm our precious pets.

There are many causes of intoxication:

- Disinfection substances: The bird has difficulty in breathing, it has discolored eyes. The bird's life is in danger!
- Soap or deodorants: They contain a substance that could lead to temporary blindness. Wash the affected area with cold water.
- Alcohol: The bird is vomiting, it has fluffy feathers, stays in the corner of the cage and is losing balance. The sick and old birds could die; a healthy bird could recover by itself.
- Toxic plants.
- Nicotine (cigarette butts): It can affect the nervous system, causing death. Don't leave cigarettes near the birds.
- Salt (and salty foods): The bird is very thirsty, is agitated and shaking. You'll need to administer lots of water through the

bird's beak and laxatives. In severe situations, the bird could die.

- Teflon (from frying pans): suffocation and death in 30 minutes. Avoid keeping the bird in the kitchen; in case of accidents remove the bird outside as fast as possible.
- Lead (newspapers, lead-based paint): green colored diarrhea (even the presence of blood), the kidneys, the bone marrow and the nervous system are affected. If the accident is discovered in time, the administration of an antidote is required - calcium EDTA (aminopolycarboxylic acid).
- Milk can be offered to alleviate the vomiting symptoms. Another solution is the administration of medicinal coal. You'll have to dissolve 5 grams of medicinal coal in 50 ml of water. This will need to be administered through the beak. Once you have carried out the operations described above, after one hour, you'll have to administer some oily purgatives, oil or castor oil.

## 11. Vitamins and minerals in excess or deficiency

Insufficient or too much vitamin intake can cause serious health problems in the birds. The owners have to assure them an optimal intake of vitamins and minerals.

### a) Vitamin A

Vitamin A deficiency is considered the main cause of diseases in caged birds. In the bird's body, carotene is transformed in vitamin A. Sources of provitamin A are fish fat or cod liver oil, egg yolk, carrots, green plants, vegetables, and sunflower seeds.

*Symptoms:*
- Drying of the surface of the eyeball
- Eyelid edema
- Infections of the mucous membranes
- Rhinitis

- Sinusitis
- White membranes inside the beak
- Kidney problems and gout (gout occurs in birds when uric acid level becomes too high in their blood stream)
- Swollen feet
- Diarrhea
- Fluffed plumage
- In the molting period, the slow growth process of feathers.

*Treatment:*
- Fish fat or cod liver oil 3-4 drops through the beak.

**b) Vitamin B complex:**

Birds can get their required vitamin B intake from cereal germs, rice bran, raw egg yolk, carrots, oranges, other fruits, fresh cottage cheese, cooked liver and beer yeast.

*Symptoms:*
- Unable to keep their head straight
- Slow growth rate
- Weight loss
- Nerve problems
- Paralysis
- Spasms
- Digestive disorders
- Diarrhea.

*Treatment:*
- Beer yeast must be dissolved in warm water before administration. The preventive doses must be administered daily, until the bird will be perfectly healthy: 5-10 years old bird must have 50 mg beer yeast/day; 11-20 years old bird must have 100-150 mg beer yeast /day; 21-30 years old bird must have 200-250 mg beer yeast/day; 31-40 years old bird must have 300-350 mg beer yeast/day; 41-50 years old bird

must have 400-450 mg beer yeast/day; 51-60 years old bird must have 500-550 mg beer yeast/day; 60-70 years old bird must have 550-600 mg beer yeast/day; 70 years old bird must have 650-800 mg beer yeast/day.

- Administration of B5 and B12 is given in liquid form, a couple of drops through the beak or in drinking water. You must add 1-2 ml of B complex in 50-100 ml of water for 3-5 days.

## c) Vitamin C

This can be found in green plants, bananas, grapes, blackcurrant, rose hips, parsley, etc.

*Symptoms:*
- The fragility of very small blood vessels
- Hematomas
- Tiredness.

*Treatment:*
- The treatment of this deficiency is as simple as feeding your bird more food rich in this vitamin or vitamin supplements.

## d) Vitamin D

This can be found in green plants, egg yolk, fish flour, beer yeast and of course the exposure of the bird to natural sunlight.

*Symptoms:*
- Slowing growth
- Fluffed plumage
- rachitis
- Bone fragility
- Calcium deposits
- Lack or softening of the egg shell.

*Treatment:*
- Administration of fish fat or cod liver oil, first a few drops through the beak, then mixed with food.

## 12.  Bird diseases which could affect humans

I will not go into the symptoms and treatment of these diseases, as you will likely see them in the bird before in yourself. Therefore, once your bird has been diagnosed with one of the following, you know it is time to get yourself checked out too.

- Tuberculosis (mycobacterium avium)
- Ornithosis
- Psittacosis
- Chlamydiosis
- Chlamydia Psittaci
- Orthomyxoviruses
- Paramyxoviruses
- Salmonella
- Klebsiella Pneumoniae.

## 13.  Viral diseases

Viruses are in a continuous transformation, and birds with other animals constitute a reservoir of viruses. There are several vaccines for birds, which helps them to fight against the viruses. The treatment of viral diseases is based on the support of vital functions of the bird and the capacity to fight viruses. Administration of vitamins, good quality food and antibiotics get rid of the symptoms.

### a) Avian pseudo pest (Newcastle disease)

The avian pseudo pest is a very contagious disease, which mostly affects backyard birds and could contaminate cage birds as well. The spread of the pseudo pest virus is facilitated by already infested wild birds (sparrows, crows, magpies). It could be spread through food, water and air.

*Symptoms:*

- Diarrhea with or without blood
- Dehydration
- Weight loss
- Breathing difficulties
- Discharge from nostrils
- Fever
- Paralysis of the legs and wings
- Anorexia
- Indigestion
- Torticollis.

*Treatment:*

- Disinfection of the cage or aviary is required.
- Vaccination of the bird, which must be given subcutaneously or intramuscularly.
- If the vaccine is administered in water, you'll have to be sure that the water, the water recipients and the cage are perfectly clean.

### b) Avian pox in cage birds

The Avipox virus could affect every backyard and aviary bird. It's also called "the suffocation disease". The evolution is very fast in youngsters, without any signs of disease. The virus can be transmitted by direct contact with infected chickens or by mosquitoes. There are at least 3 different types of Avipox Viruses: fowl pox viruses (chickens, turkeys, peacocks, pheasants), pigeon poxviruses and canary pox viruses (canaries, sparrows).

*Symptoms:*

- Breathing through an open beak
- Conjunctivitis
- Catarrh.

- There is a cutaneous form which appears as yellowish nodules on the eyelids, around the nose, cloaca and inside the wings.

*Treatment:*
- Administration of a vaccine is required which has to be given every year.
- Avipoxvirus is very resistant in the dark and can survive 14 days at 38 degrees Celsius (100,4 degrees Fahrenheit), 15 months at room temperature and 5 minutes at 100 degrees Celsius (212 degrees Fahrenheit). It can be destroyed with caustic soda 1-2%.

## c) Pacheco's disease
This is caused by a group of psittacine herpesviruses and is a highly contagious disease, with incubation period of 3-14 days, causing sudden death.

*Symptoms:*
- Lack of appetite
- Diarrhea
- White-yellowish droppings with blood in it.
- Sometimes they present conjunctivitis, sinusitis and loss of balance.

*Treatment:*
- An antiviral drug (Acyclovir) followed by supportive treatments can reduce death rates in other exposed birds.

## d) Marek's disease
This is an infectious disease caused by a virus from the Herpesviridae family, which resists 7 days in feces, up to 16 weeks in bedding and 6 weeks in dust particles. Marek's disease is a type of avian cancer which most commonly affects the backyard birds.

*Symptoms:*
- Tumors can occur in the eyes and cause irregularly shaped pupils and blindness. Tumors of the kidneys, liver, pancreas and muscles can cause lack of coordination.
- Paleness
- Weak, labored breathing.

*Treatment:*
- The birds can be vaccinated against tumor formation, but does not prevent the infection with the virus. Marek's virus is transmitted by the air and it also affects the respiratory and digestive system.
- Birds exposed to Marek's disease are considered carriers for life, even if they were previously vaccinated.

# 14. Bacterial diseases
## a) Avian respiratory mycoplasmosis
This is a chronic infectious disease that can be found in chickens, turkeys, pheasants, quails, peacocks, etc.

*Symptoms:*
- In youngsters of 2-3 days old the symptoms are characterized by respiratory problems and conjunctivitis and it has a slow evolution.
- At adult birds it is characterized by weight loss and respiratory disorders.
- Stagnation in developing
- Sneeze and cough
- Open beak breathing
- Sinusitis
- Enteritis
- Lack of appetite
- Respiratory disorders.

*Treatment:*

- To combat mycoplasmosis, the sick birds have to be isolated and those that are apparently healthy have to be preventively treated with antibiotics.
- Terramycin administered subcutaneously in superior part of the neck. After the administration of injection with Terramycin a local reaction will appear and will usually disappear after 10-14 days.
- Oxytetracycline or Streptomycin for 3 days or Erythromycin intramuscularly for 5-7 days.
- Administration of vitamins in drinking water or feed is also recommended.

## b) Pasteurellosis

Thi is an infection caused by a bacteria called Pasteurella, which is found in humans and animals as well. The infection could spread through droppings and saliva of animals. It affects mostly adult birds.

*Symptoms:*

- Fever
- Tiredness
- Presence of mucous in droppings.

*Treatment:*

- Chloramphenicol
- Oxytetracycline
- Tetracycline.

## c) Psittacosis or parrot fever

This is caused by a bacteria called Chlamydia psittaci and it can be identified in more than 130 species of birds: parrots, canaries, pigeons, geese, ducks, turkeys, chickens, pheasants, doves, seagulls, etc.

*Symptoms:*

- Lack of appetite
- Weight loss
- Tiredness
- Conjunctivitis
- Fever
- Respiratory disorders
- White-green or bloody colored diarrhea
- The sick bird may shiver
- Lethargy
- Discharge from the nose and eyes.

**Treatment:**

- To combat disease separate the sick birds from healthy ones and disinfect the cage. You must use protection equipment to avoid infestation. After this process the protection equipment has to be sterilized.
- The affected birds have to be treated with Tetracycline or Doxycycline for 3 weeks.

## 15. How to administer medication to your parrot

There are a few possible methods you can take up when administering medication to your parrot:

### *Adding medication to drinking water*

Adding medication in drinking water is a controversial method, but sometimes this is the only available method. The purpose is for the bird to take the medicine during the day directly from the drinking water. There are lots of disadvantages of this method. The bitter taste of the water makes the bird to refuse to drink it. Some birds will refuse to drink water if its color has changed. Another disadvantage is that the water-medicine mixture has to be prepared and changed daily. There is a risk that your bird could dehydrate.

### Adding medication in food

This method is better than the one with water, because you can hide the medicine in the favorite food of your parrot. Usually you can mix suspensions (liquid medicines), tablets or the content of a capsule in food.

The disadvantage of this method is that the bird could refuse to eat the food mixed with medicine, because it changed the food taste. It could be difficult to mix the medicine with the food because of the hard consistency of the medicine, and could be needed to add some water to soften the medicine. The other disadvantage is, if there are several birds in the cage, all the others may eat from the medicine-food mixture.

### Liquid medication (suspensions)

This is the best method to administer liquid medication to your bird directly through the beak. Most oral suspensions are accepted very well by the birds, especially those with a good taste. You'll have to follow the follwing procedure:

- Fill the syringe or pipette with the prescribed quantity of suspension. There should be no needle on the syringe.

- Before you try restraining your bird, it's worth seeing if s/he will accept the suspension from the syringe through the cage bars. If not, you'll have to take out your parrot from its cage and wrap it in a towel, only the head and the chest of the bird will be uncovered and the chest also needs to be able to rise and fall in order for your bird to breathe.

- Before you start to administer the suspension, you'll have to wait until the bird calms down.

- You'll have to place the syringe at the left or right side of the beak, (it's possible that bird will bite it at first) and after you

106

managed to place it in the interior of the beak, you can administer the suspension very slowly.

- Allow the bird to swallow frequently, because if you squeeze the suspension too fast, the medicine can get into the lungs and the bird could die.

- It's possible to observe that the suspension is getting out through the nostrils of the bird. Don't panic, just stop giving any medicine to your bird and leave it to calm down. Call your vet to help.

*Injectable medications*
Another method for administering medication is through repeated injections. Usually this kind of method is not used very often, (only in emergency cases) because the bird is exposed to repeated stress because of the pain. You should never give injections yourself though; this is a vet's job.

## 16. When to See an Avian Vet
Every minor symptom your bird exhibits doesn't require a costly visit to the vet. There are certain signs to watch out for, however, that signal a bigger problem than a bad mood.

Consult an avian vet when you notice these symptoms in your cockatiel:
- Loss of appetite lasting more than a couple of days.
- An untidy appearance despite proper grooming habits.
- Excessive feather plucking.
- Abnormal droppings.
- Disorientation.
- Excessive drinking.
- Odd sleep behavior.

- Change in normal activities like playing, talking or bonding with humans.
- Changes in energy levels.
- Soiled tail, wings or bottom.

**Tip**: Making it a habit to check your pet's appearance and behavior every day will help you greatly in being aware when something is wrong. You'll be able to spot changes in your bird's behavior early on, before problems escalate.

# Chapter 5. Breeding Cockatiels: Is It a Wise Choice?

Some people decide to keep cockatiels in order to make a business out of breeding ands selling them as pets. If you are one of those people, read on to find out useful tips and facts about cockatiel breeding.

**Breeding**

Cockatiels reach sexual maturity at 1½ - 2 years old. They are usually reproducing all year long, but most of them are likely to do so in winter or at the beginning of spring. Breeding season takes place during the months of March and April. Cockatiels mate for life. During summer, you should separate your birds, (males from females), because their hatchlings will not tolerate extreme heat, which raises their risks of health problems.

They will breed in shadowy places or in nesting boxes. Hens usually lay between 3-8 eggs, and the egg-sitting period lasts for 21 days. The weaning period of the youngsters takes place between 6-7 weeks old. The hatchlings are blind and naked. The pair will need to be provided with plenty of food, especially soft food to allow them to feed their youngsters. As the parents get ready for their next breeding season, after 6 months (or longer) the youngsters will need to be removed from the nesting box.

If you are not sure about your youngest parrot gender, then you should introduce an adult male among youngsters. The male will recognize and will stay close to the preferred female. Once they mate, you can remove the new pair into another aviary or a separate place.

Cockatiels require nesting boxes with dimensions of 7.87 x 7.87 x 9.84 inches (20 x 20 x 25cm) and the entrance hole should be 6cm in diameter.

The nesting box should have a removable top lid for nest inspection. Nesting materials such as pine or wood shavings and dried plant materials should cover the bottom of the nest box. Double entrance boxes are often used to reduce the chance of the male trapping the female in the nesting box. During breeding season, males become aggressive, so clipping their wings will help the females to escape.

### Choosing Cockatiels for Breeding

If you're able to breed responsibly and feel inclined to do so, it's vital to select healthy, fully-grown cockatiels that are not related to one another. You may request a pre-breeding health test on breeding pairs performed by an avian vet. This may include both gram stains and blood tests. The tests will help determine if the cockatiels come with sub-clinical infections or deficiencies in nutrition.

You will also have to factor in the age of the birds. Don't breed cockatiels younger than 18 months old. Even though young birds may be able to perform the mating act, young cockatiel males can be infertile and possibly injure the young female birds through health issues like egg binding. Furthermore, choosing cockatiel parents that are too young takes away nutrients these growing pets need. Chicks born from parents that are not ready to breed are typically weaker than the offspring produced by fully grown cockatiels.

It's never a good idea to breed birds that are related to one another. Doing so leads to chicks born with birth defects and a myriad of other potential health problems. It's not uncommon for cockatiels born from related parents to have physical abnormalities such as deformed beaks. They may even be born with missing body parts. Other issues that can arise are deformed or missing wings, toes or legs, orthopedic health problems that will negatively affect the cockatiel's ability to fly, climb, perch or walk, malfunctioning organs and infertility. Inbreeding can also lead to decreased egg-production, infertile eggs or a lower rate of eggs that hatch. Choose to breed only fully-grown and healthy cockatiels that come from different bloodlines.

**Laying the Eggs**
Female cockatiels lay eggs seven to ten days after a successful mating session. It's normal for the females to lay an egg every 48 hours. A group of cockatiel eggs laid at once is called a "clutch". Clutches usually come in two to eight eggs.

Prior to your cockatiel laying an egg and while it's laying, the bird will emit extra-large and smelly droppings. Don't worry, as this is completely normal. There are also cases when parent cockatiels will wait until two or three eggs are laid before they begin nesting. The reason the birds wait for a bit is so that the majority of the eggs will hatch at about the same time. Eggs only begin to incubate after the parents nest on them, getting the eggs warm. Cockatiel eggs stay viable for up to a week before nesting is essential. If your parent cockatiels hesitate to enter a nesting box, it may help to hang a strip of millet seed close to the entrance of the nesting box.

Expect the cockatiel eggs to hatch 18 to 21 days after the parents begin to nest. A few days prior to hatching, there is an air cell found at the wider end of each egg that will increase in size and begin to tilt. The chick will then move about, moving the air cell in the process. This step is known as "drawdown".

When the chick is located inside the air cell, it will begin to breathe using its lungs. The baby will increasingly act more active, using up the oxygen found inside the cell. As the carbon dioxide levels rise, the chick's neck and abdominal muscles will start to contract. These contractions will then push the baby bird's back against its shell, leading the chick's feet to push against the opposite end of the shell. Thanks to the muscle contractions in the neck area of the bird, the "egg tooth" found inside the baby's beak will begin to puncture and break the inner shell.

Keep an eye out for the initial visible sign of hatching: the external pip mark. It will look like a tiny dent or bump that comes with small cracks found on the external side of the shell. This mark will grow in size as the chick breaks off the shell. When the shell is punctured and the cockatiel chick begins to breathe the air outside, you might hear some vocalization.

**Newborn Cockatiels**
Make sure you visually observe each chick as soon as it has hatched. A healthy baby cockatiel should have yellow-pink skin and the bird should feel warm.

When a chick is dehydrated, it will appear wrinkled and skinny. Their skin will look dry and red or muddy in color, while the skin will feel sticky when touched. Always take dehydration in your pets seriously.

Dehydration is a very serious problem when it occurs in newly hatched chicks. If a baby cockatiel comes out dehydrated, give it a drop of warm Pedialyte. Do not repeat the process unless you observe the liquid go through the baby's beak and the bird has passed at least one dropping.

Some professional breeders will regularly provide baby cockatiels a drop of warm Pedialyte as soon as the birds hatch. This is to avoid dehydration. Once a normal dropping has passed, the drops are given every hour. By instinct, cockatiel parents will take away pieces of eggshell from their chicks right after they hatch. As soon as they're done, the chick should look fluffy and clean.

Remove the empty eggshells from the nesting box as soon as you can. Failure to do so can lead to bacterial growth. Cockatiel parents might wait up to eight hours before feeding their chicks for the first time. They usually wait to allow the babies to dry. Nature will provide nutrition to the chicks via the yolk sac. This sac is absorbed before the hatching gets completed.

**How to hand feed a baby parrot**
The maximum quantity that has to be given to a baby parrot before the weaning period has to be 10% of its body weight. The crop of most baby parrots usually gets empty between 4-6 hours. You'll have to stop feeding the bird during nighttime, between midnight and 6 o'clock, which will allow the crop to empty of residual food. As the baby parrot grows, you'll have to reduce the number of feeding times, but you'll have to increase a little bit more the quantity of food.

The most important thing is to control the quantity of food offered at each meal. Don't offer more food than 10% of the bird's body weight in a meal. As the baby parrot grows, it will refuse to be hand feed and you'll have to stop with hand feeding or you'll have to reduce them. When you are at the stage of only 2-3 hand feedings, offer your bird solid food (softened pellets) or cooked food. In 2-3 weeks' time, your bird should be able to get used to solid food and you can completely skip the evening meals.

*How to prepare the hand feeding formula*
- Use commercially-prepared hand feeding formula which is specifically created for cockatiel babies.

- You should use a thermometer to ensure that the hand feeding formula is warm enough (about 102 to 105 degrees Fahrenheit).

- Use the microwave to heat up the water, add a measured amount of formula and stir. Make sure you feed at the right temperature.

- Baby parrots develop much better on thin formula rather than a thick one.

- There are two most common methods of feeding: by syringe or spoon.

- Allow the bird to breath between bites of food and stop feeding when the crop is nicely rounded. You can feed this formula up to 7 weeks of age.

At this time you can start introducing weaning food in the bird's diet. Start weaning your baby with veggies, seeds, fruits and good quality pellets. Grains and sprouted seeds are also a good start in weaning your baby parrot, because the softened shell is easier to break. Place a separate water dish next to his food. Any remains must be removed after 3 hours. At 9-10 weeks of age your baby parrot should be placed on a single feeding per day. At this time pellets and seed mix should be its favorite food. Serve fruits and veggies cut in small pieces. You can serve warm, moistened pellets early in the morning at 8am and 4pm.

At the age of 12 weeks old your bird should be eating on its own. During the weaning period some babies can lose up to 15% of their weight.

It is important to keep an eye on your young bird regularly regarding feeding. Watch your young bird's weight until it is 5 months old. Take your bird in your hand at least once a day and feel its breastbone by moving your hand from side to side across his/her chest. A healthy young cockatiel should have its breastbone covered with soft muscles on each side of it. When you want to bring home a young cockatiel, make sure the feed pots are placed on the bottom of the cage. Their climbing skills are not yet developed and so the easiest way to feed themselves will be from the pots placed on the bottom of the cage. Set up the cage with the perches placed down low, until your bird learns to climb around.

Other foods can also be offered to your baby, like chopped hardboiled egg, scrambled egg, chopped roast chicken breast, white boneless fish, boiled rice or pasta, biscuit crumbs, millet spray, boiled sweet potato mash.

Here is a delicious recipe for young cockatiels:
- 1 and 1/2 cups fresh corn
- 1 cup brown rice
- 1/2 cup dried mango or banana
- 2 and 1/2 tbsp. raisins
- 3 and 1/2 tbsp. split lentils or peas
- 2 and 1/2 tbsp. unsalted pistachio nuts
- 1 tsp dried powdered milk.

Bring 0.5 liters of water to boil, add all contents, cover and boil gently for 30 minutes. Serve warm or cool.

For pet owners who work full-time, breeding is definitely discouraged. While cockatiel chicks are absolutely adorable, like human newborn babies, they are also absolutely helpless and dependent right after they hatch.

Cockatiel chicks greet the world naked and their eyes are completely closed. These newborns are utterly dependent on parent cockatiels for food, warmth and survival. Bear in mind that the life of a cockatiel chick is your responsibility, should you decide to become a breeder. You also have the task of caring for the cockatiel parents, including looking at their progress after the fertilized eggs have hatched. You'll need to monitor the health of mother and father cockatiels.

It's not rare for parent and baby cockatiels to experience health issues that will require the services of an avian vet. If budget restrictions keep you from being able to afford a vet's services, it's best not to even think about breeding any kind of bird. It would be irresponsible to commit to breeding without having enough resources to cover veterinary expenses.

# Conclusion

Thank you for buying this book. I hope it has answered all your burning questions regarding cockatiel care, breeding, feeding, health problems and many more.

I hope you have realized that, although owning a cockatiel can be hard work, this will pay off when you see what a wander it is to own this beautiful, docile, playful animal as a pet.

Printed in Great Britain
by Amazon

52648329R00068